Voices from the Hospice

Voices from the Hospice

Staying with life through Suffering and Waiting

Bob Whorton

scm press

© Bob Whorton 2015

Published in 2015 by SCM Press
Editorial office
3rd Floor
Invicta House
108–114 Golden Lane,
London EC1Y 0TG

SCM Press is an imprint of Hymns Ancient & Modern Ltd
(a registered charity)
13A Hellesdon Park Road
Norwich NR6 5DR, UK

www.scmpress.co.uk

978-0-334-05426-9

All biblical quotations are from the New Revised Standard Version
Bible: Anglicized Edition, copyright 1989, 1995, Division of Christian
Education of the National Council of the Churches of Christ in the
United States of America. Used by permission. All rights reserved.

Typeset by Manila Typesetting Company
Printed and bound by CPI Group (UK) Ltd, Croydon

Dedication

*To all the patients, family members and
friends, staff and volunteers
at Sobell House Hospice who have been so
much part of my life
over these last nine years.*

Contents

ORIENTATION
DISORIENTATION
NEW ORIENTATION

Acknowledgements

I would like to express my grateful thanks to those who have helped me in the preparation of *Voices from the Hospice*:

My thanks go to Margaret Whipp and Louise Adey-Huish for their careful reading of the original text and their helpful suggestions; to Joanna Tulloch for her poem 'Conveyancing', which was such a gift when I read it; to Phillip Whorton for a specific piece of editing work with the biblical passages; to Irene Ertl, a patient who attends the day services at Sobell House, who believed that this writing should and would be published; to Natalie Watson at SCM Press for being a willing midwife in this book's birth; and finally, heartfelt thanks to Isabel Gregory who has encouraged me to stay with my own soul journey and to Jessica Osborne who has been a patient and wise supervisor.

Introduction

A train journey is different from a car journey. In a car we can easily stop or change our route, and we are driving ourselves to the destination. We can hold firmly on to the steering wheel and feel we are in control of the journey. But when we travel by train, we buy a ticket and travel through all the stations until we arrive at our destination. We have to trust the train driver to take us there.

Many of us would like to find short cuts on the track that leads to spiritual life. We would prefer not to have to travel through each of the stations in turn. And I suspect many of us want the journey to be different from how it actually is. Secretly, we think we would be better off without our particular family and the colleagues we work with. We think we would flourish in a different sort of job rather than the one we actually do. How much easier it would be if we could build our own spiritual house, rather than having it built for us to someone else's design. We want transformation to be under our own control, and we would prefer not to have it at all if it means receiving the terrible gifts of failure and the undermining of ego.

But, what if there is a necessary suffering[1] and necessary 'deaths' on this track to life? What if we were to discover an empty place where something new could grow, rather than a place so crammed with our ego and projects and desire to keep

---

1 For this helpful phrase, see Richard Rohr, *Falling Upwards: A Spirituality for the Two Halves of Life*, San Francisco: Jossey-Bass, 2011, Ch. 6.

moving, that nothing ever seems to change. We need a new orientation which for many of us comes out of the failure of our normal life. A new platform must be provided for us to stand on. Joanna Tulloch, a poet and Methodist local preacher, suggests in this poem about resurrection that the way to life is 'to stay on the train' until it takes us to where we need to be. It was this poem that helped me to bring together the ideas for this book.

Conveyancing

The invitation is to a new home,
a renewed body,
and a rising, rising up
out of the harrowing of hell.
The door to this new house
will open
in its own time,
in God's own time,
and it's no good
trying to short-circuit the process.
The train that takes us there
stops at every station,
all those crowded platforms
of shouting people
at first waving palms
but later their fists.
And the last stop, on Friday,
is deserted.
It comes in the night-time
of the day-time,
when the curtain is torn in two
and there seems to be
no protection, just abandonment.
All will seem lost
as God pays the price of love,
but in that very moment

we have redemption,
we have completion,
and something is conveyed
that the world has
never seen before.
The key to the new life
is forged from iron nails,
placed in the lock by the one
they mock,
and turned three times.
After that, no more looking
through the keyhole,
for the invitation is to
a new body,
a new life –
Come in, and make yourself
at home.

Joanna Tulloch[2]

This is how it was for Christ in his passion, death and resurrection, and this is how it is for us. The terrible truth is that there are no short cuts. There really aren't. We cannot skip merrily into resurrection without walking the way of the cross first. I have had some crunching failures in my time which I would prefer to un-live. But these are some of the stations I have needed to travel through. It seems that many of us fail precisely in the place where we do not wish to fail, and these shameful, unwanted places are all necessary stations on the way.

I work as a hospice chaplain at Sir Michael Sobell House Hospice in Oxford. The track followed by those who come to the hospice is inevitably a hard one. Some people will come willingly to the hospice ward for the control of their symptoms and go home again. Some come through the doors unwillingly, fearing that this might be the final station of this life, and not

---

2 J. Tulloch, *A Reflection of God*, Leicester: Matador Publishing, 2014, p. 67.

wishing it to be. Some know that they are nearly there and are glad. For those living with cancer the train is likely to have stopped at many different stations on the way: diagnosis, chemotherapy, radiotherapy, coping with physical and spiritual distress and negotiating difficult conversations. Sometimes they have been able to get out of the train, have a cup of tea and enjoy the surrounding countryside for a while. But then the train moves on, and they have to be on it. I see this in people's eyes, and I wonder who it is harder for – the person who is dying or the family who stay and watch and love?

For most of us it is very hard indeed when we are not in control of our living. We may have a family member who needs our time and care; we have an addiction which we cannot fully admit to; we are trapped in a job which does not fulfil us; we are in a suffocating relationship; we live with illness, disability or depression; we are not on the spiritual path we want to be on. If only the train driver would take us somewhere else! But the train keeps going through the 'wrong' stations.

There are of course times when we need to take control. We may need to seek outside help with the challenges we are facing, or we may need to change our job or leave a relationship. But, there are some things that simply need to be lived. We need a discerning heart to know what needs to be changed by our own courageous action and what needs to be patiently lived. Can we let ourselves be taken to some stations (and also some station waiting rooms) which are not of our choosing, knowing that the way we travel is the track to life? In one of the most challenging verses in the Gospels, the risen Christ says to Peter at the end of his conversation with him at the lakeside:

'Very truly, I tell you, when you were younger, you used to fasten your own belt and to go wherever you wished. But when you grow old, you will stretch out your hands, and someone else will fasten a belt around you and take you where you do not wish to go.' (John 21.18)

In this book I am going to draw upon the rich resource of the songs contained in the book of Psalms in the Old Testament. These songs have been used for centuries in the worship of Israel and in the Christian Church, but they have a startling immediacy today, and a spiritual honesty which is quite refreshing. I have come to appreciate the psalms later on in my life: for years I dismissed many of them because I saw there only violence and lack of forgiveness towards 'the enemy'. I now see that these songs speak powerfully of the struggle between life and death in the soul. They will help us to stay on the track.

The Temple of Solomon was destroyed in 566 BC and the Second Temple was dedicated in 516 BC after the return from exile in Babylon. The book of Psalms became the songbook of this Second Temple. Guilds of singers transmitted these songs through the generations, respecting the ancient material while making adaptations to fit new circumstances. We can detect a core of early material embedded in them and can be reasonably sure that these songs have their origins reaching far back into the history of the Jewish people.

A brief survey of the most significant students of the psalms may be helpful. In the first part of the twentieth century Hermann Gunkel used the new tool of form criticism to analyse the psalms. He found that certain of these songs (but not all) had similar characteristics, modes of speech and apparent uses and could be grouped together. His categorization is still widely used today. Hermann Gunkel[3] discovered hymns, laments, royal psalms, wisdom poems, psalms of thanksgiving and pilgrimage songs, and he developed theories about how these psalms were used in the religion of Israel. The Norwegian scholar Sigmund Mowinckel[4] came to believe that more than 40 psalms were directly linked to an enthronement festival at the autumn festival. The well-being of the nation was directly related to the

---

3 Hermann Gunkel and Joachim Begrich, *An Introduction to the Psalms*, Macon, GA: Mercer University Press (1926) 1998.

4 Sigmund Mowinckel, *The Psalms in Israel's Worship*, Grand Rapids, MI: Eerdmans (1962) 2004.

strength and well-being of the Davidic king, and in many psalms Mowinckel saw evidence of a ceremony in which the king was clothed again with power under the kingship of God. This was, and remains, a controversial theory, but one that has not gone away. Claus Westermann[5] focused on the lament psalm as the most important of the forms. He examined the movement in the lament psalm from alienation and abandonment to praise and thanksgiving and saw this movement as fundamental to the psalms and to the whole faith of Israel. As we shall see, Walter Brueggemann[6] has taken these ideas and developed them in a creative and compelling way. When I was at theological college in Birmingham, we were guided through the Old Testament by John H. Eaton.[7] I have found his studies on the psalms very helpful and his book *Psalms of Life* is both scholarly and devotional. I will also refer to William P. Brown's interesting book *Seeing the Psalms*.[8] This is a detailed study of the use of imagery and metaphors in the psalms. Unless otherwise indicated, the translation of the Bible I have used is the New Revised Standard Version.

Here is a brief summary of the track ahead:

In order to find our true way to spiritual life, many of us will need to travel through some hard 'stations' and endure some frustrating times waiting for the next train. There are no short cuts. We will need to face 'death' in its many forms and our culture does not prepare us for this. However, in the hospice people live this journey every day and they can be our teachers. The songs we know as psalms express the wisdom we need and will also guide us on the way. By allowing ourselves to be taken on this journey we will find life.

---

5 Claus Westermann, *Praise and Lament in the Psalms*, Louisville, KY: Westminster John Knox Press, 1987.

6 Walter Brueggemann, *The Message of the Psalms: A Theological Commentary*, Minneapolis, MN: Augsburg, 1984.

7 John H. Eaton, *Psalms*, London: SCM Press, 1967, and *Psalms for Life*, London: SPCK, 2006.

8 William P. Brown, *Seeing the Psalms: A Theology of Metaphor*, Louisville, KY: Westminster John Knox Press, 2002.

In the book you will find there is a three-way 'conversation' taking place between the singers of psalms, my own soul and the voices of patients and relatives in the hospice. (In order to protect confidentiality I have changed names and significant details, while still keeping the essential meaning of what was being expressed. The exceptions to this are Pete in Chapter 3, who gave me permission to share his story, Val in Chapter 12, who was such a definite person that I cannot give her a different name, and Lorraine Long in the Postscript, whose family have given me their permission to use her writing.) In Chapters 1 to 4 we will explore the way to spiritual life and the curious manner in which it may be found. Chapters 5 to 8 take us through some of the stations we may well have to pass through en route. In Chapters 9 to 11 we will examine some station waiting rooms. Chapter 12 reminds us we cannot do this journey alone, and Chapter 13 concludes with some thoughts about allowing the process of death and life in us.

I

Living with Uncertainty

I hate it when I am not in control of my days. I do not know what I will have to face when I walk into the hospice. When I am as fresh as a daisy this can be quite exciting, but when I have absorbed too much distress and I am tired through to my bones, I can be filled with anxiety. Will I be OK? Will I get 'it' right, or will I do something stupid? Will I cope with even more human suffering? And I hate it when I do not know what the future holds. I am beginning to think of life when I leave the hospice. I catch myself thinking about what sort of 'leaving do' I would like to have. There are times when I seem to prefer living in the future rather than in the present, and this is strange considering the fact that I want to be here for at least another year! I want to know how I will get through this time and what will come after. But so many things could happen in the intervening period. I don't know what my health will be like, and I don't know about the needs of my family. I don't know what the financial market will be like when we come to sell the house. I don't know if we will move abroad or continue to live in this country. I don't know what work I'll be doing. I don't know, and I hate the not knowing.

A stable life?

We human beings do not live comfortably with uncertainty. We like to know what we will be doing tomorrow, next week and next year. This gives us a sense of security. And most of us need our habits. The habit of getting up in the morning and going off to work is one which can be very helpful. Holidays can be very stressful times for some of us, because we have to make endless decisions about what to do and where to go! And in the western world we live with a set of unquestioned assumptions: we will not be hungry or thirsty, we will have a decent standard of living, diseases can be cured and death exists only on a distant horizon.

Reading through the psalms we discover a very different world. These songs were written in a time when existence was poised between life and death, blessing and curse. Crops might grow or fail, the herd could be wiped out by drought or disease, and life was lived on the edge. People could fall off that edge quite easily, and death, with no hope of anything substantial beyond it, was ever present. Psalm 107 is a beautiful song in which desperate human need is met by God's grace. Some suffer real hunger and real thirst in desert lands (v. 5); some are held prisoner in darkness, held fast with iron bonds (v. 10); some have become ill, loathing the sight of food, and at the very gates of death (v. 18); some go to sea and have to endure the terrors of wind and storm (v. 23ff.) The psalm shows how easily our stable, 'normal' life can be turned upside down; according to the singer, it is only by 'crying to the Lord' that people can be saved from their troubles.

The purpose of Temple worship was not to grow a private spirituality, rather it was the means by which life itself could continue for the whole community. In this community worship, life was renewed and blessing ensured. Through words, clapping, ritual acts and dancing, the people were creating a new reality of righteousness, blessing and salvation. The Davidic king, representing the King of all creation, had a special role in making this reality anew. And within this worship the psalms had a central place. They expressed the soul of the nation, reaching out in joy and pain to Yahweh, their God. In the middle of an uncertain life poised between life and death, God was the ground on which they could stand.

Some stories

The journey through cancer care and onwards to palliative care is one that nobody chooses. The names of the stations are unknown, until they are travelled through. The waiting rooms are numerous. This journey is characterized by uncertainty and the following stories are typical of those who travel on this special train:

> Julie was sitting on the comfortable chair alongside her bed on the oncology ward. She was trying to read a book, but told me she was reading the same page over and over again. She was waiting for a doctor to come and give the results of her latest scan. She did not look at me as she talked: 'What will the cancer markers reveal? I suspect the cancer has spread, but I don't know until someone tells me. Will they say I need more chemo? Here's the doctor now . . .'

> Gill came to our day services because her specialist nurse was concerned about Gill's growing isolation. Her cancer treatments had left her fatigued and low in mood. She had enjoyed her work as an administrator at one of the Oxford colleges, but now she was stuck at home feeling tired, ill and miserable. She and her husband had considerable debts, and she was very anxious about their financial situation. She said to me, 'I'm not concerned about myself but about those I'm leaving behind. How is my husband going to cope when I've died?'

> Ken was about to move to Sobell House from a ward where active treatments were the norm. When I went to see him he was full of anxieties and many, many questions. 'What is it going to be like moving to a hospice? Can I still have some treatments or will they just leave me to die? It's supposed to be a lovely place but I'm not sure I want to go there, because if I go there, I will finally have to face the fact that I am going

to die – and die fairly soon. I'm not sure about this, it feels so final. What is dying going to be like? I'm scared.'

When I met Sarah on our hospice ward, she told me what it was like to live with a brain tumour. Of all cancers these are the most unpredictable. She was 'given' 3 months to live 18 months ago and said: 'There is something hanging over me all the time. It's a bit like living on death row, not knowing when you are going to be called to face death.'

David was a very religious man. He found his faith enormously helpful, and when he came into the hospice, he was eager to tell me that he was a Christian. He wanted his illness to glorify God and to be a witness to the gospel as he was dying. As a chaplain, I wanted to support David in his faith, but I was also worried for him. I was concerned that he might be tempted to play down any fears, uncertainties or negativity that crept into his soul. He very much wanted to 'keep strong' and to keep hold of his faith. This meant denying all weakness and natural worry about dying. At first, David was unremittingly cheerful with all his visitors and all of the staff team. He had come into the hospice to die, and he was determined to die praising God. But as the days went by, and he found himself to be still alive, he became less sure of the track he was following. His symptoms became more and more challenging, and he seemed to lose his bearings. David was cast down into a deep depression. He tried to remain cheerful with the nurses, but it was obviously taking a huge effort. He did not want to see his church friends and struggled to talk to his family. One day he told me that he feared losing his faith altogether.

Diana had been coming to our day services for about a year. She owned an antiques shop in a village outside Oxford and had been trying to sell it. Diana put her all into this business and became very upset when people came round to view it and saw it as 'just a business'. The sale had recently fallen through, and this was devastating for her. Normally she would cope with such things, but Diana was exhausted after years of treatment for her cancer. Would she be able to find another buyer? When she talked to me about this, I wondered out loud whether this uncertainty was a metaphor for her whole life at that moment. She began to cry. Diana told me of her elderly mother who had short-term memory problems and how concerned she was about her; she talked about her daughter living in the States whose marriage was breaking up; and finally she spoke of the last conversation with her consultant where she was given some treatment options. She did not know whether to go on another trial drug or call it a day. When she was on the previous drug regime, she did not do well and ended up feeling wretched on the oncology ward. She did not know what to do. As I listened to her, I felt helpless in the face of so many issues, and I am sure that my inner sense of helplessness was a mirror of her own feelings. All I could do was acknowledge how tough her situation was at that moment and ask her what support she had to help her through all of these challenges. She was silent for a few moments. And then, having wiped her eyes with a tissue, she lifted up her eyes, grinned at me and said, 'I suppose there is always Him Upstairs.'

Arthur came onto the hospice ward when his elderly wife found she could no longer care for him. He was asking for 'someone to put me out of my misery'. His family were expecting him to die quite quickly, but after a few days Arthur was eating again, taking medication which suited him much better and feeling quite well. Days turned into weeks, and medically there was nothing more to be done for Arthur. A hospice is a place of specialist care, and it was felt that Arthur could be cared for just as well somewhere else. So, one of the hospice social workers began some delicate conversations with Arthur and his family. Arthur was consumed with worry. He had got used to the hospice ward and was popular with the nursing team. Arthur told me, 'I want to stay here. I've settled in here, but they want to kick me out. I don't know what to do. Do I go back home with carers coming in all the time? Can my wife cope with me being back home? Our downstairs room would be turned into a hospital ward by the sound of it. Or do I go into a nursing home? I've never wanted to go into a home but that would take the pressure off my wife . . . I just don't know what to do.'

I have deliberately placed these stories one after the other. The uncertainties faced by those living with a life-limiting illness are many and various. And, of course, those of us who are not facing the end of our lives imminently (so far as we know) deceive ourselves if we think we are driving the train. We have no idea what tomorrow will bring. We just pretend to be in control of our days! How is it possible to stay with life when we do not know where the journey will take us? How can we go through the stations one by one, trusting that the train will take us where we need to go?

An earthquake

Psalm 60 contains a strange mixture of fighting language and defeat. This is a song of lament after a national defeat in which the people are thrown into crisis:

> O God, you have rejected us, broken our defences;
>> you have been angry; now restore us!
> You have caused the land to quake; you have torn it open;
>> repair the cracks in it, for it is tottering.
> You have made your people suffer hard things;
>> you have given us wine to drink that made us reel . . .

> 'With exultation I will divide up Shechem,
>> and portion out the Vale of Succoth.
> Gilead is mine, and Manasseh is mine;
>> Ephraim is my helmet;

Judah is my sceptre.
Moab is my wash-basin;
  on Edom I hurl my shoe;
  over Philistia I shout in triumph.'

Who will bring me to the fortified city?
  Who will lead me to Edom?
Have you not rejected us, O God?
  You do not go out, O God, with our armies.
O grant us help against the foe,
  for human help is worthless. With God we shall do, valiantly;
  it is he who will tread down our foes. (Psalm 60.1–3, 6b–12)

The opening lines of this song reveal a shocking situation. God has turned against his own people and this is like the land being torn apart by an earthquake. The people saw themselves as fighting for God against his enemies, but now God seems to have rejected his chosen ones. They stagger like people who have been given strong wine to drink, and there is no longer any solid ground beneath their feet. We might imagine a pause in the song, and then comes a response to this calamity. God's voice is heard in the form of a poem handed down from previous generations. The poem speaks of God as a great warrior king establishing rule over the land of Israel. This great God will surely establish victory again for his people. Moab will become his wash-basin, a land humbled and made to serve Israel (the mountains of Moab may have looked like the rim of a great bowl). He will hurl his shoe over Edom: a shoe might pick up all sorts of unpleasant residues from the ground and to this day, in many cultures, throwing a shoe at someone is a powerful sign of contempt. The message is clearly that God is on the move, like a warrior of old. But the final lines of the song return to that fearful sense of rejection. There is a crisis of faith because God does not seem to go out with the armies of Israel any more: how do they stand now with their God? The militaristic language may get in the way for us and we may need to remind ourselves that the living God is not a warrior encouraging people to fight for land. But if we can find a way through this strange language we may discover a familiar state of affairs. A crisis or tragedy occurs and the normal rules no longer apply. We are left in a state of confusion asking, 'What is going on?'

Let it be one thing or the other

I once had a very strange dream. I saw very clearly a beautiful chalice. I watched, and then the chalice 'turned on me' and was trying to destroy me. The chalice, summoning up images of the Holy Grail, is a symbol for me of plenty, life and grace. But in my dream what is life-giving turned into its opposite. I have spent a long time wondering about the meaning of this dream.

The relationship which someone has with their cancer is a complicated one. The language of battles, fighting and winning is well used, but also there may be expressions of despair and defeat. A person, not surprisingly, says, 'This is not going to beat me. I'm going to fight it.' But in their lowest moments the same person might declare, 'I've nothing left. I just want to give up.' The cry of the heart may well be, 'Let it be life or death, one or the other, but not this dreadful in-between state.' It is very hard to live in the uncertainty between these two extremes, where a person muddles along gloriously the best they can. In terms of the faith journey the extremes might be expressed as: God is/God is not; I am in the heights of ecstasy/I am abandoned by God; I am holy/I am a miserable sinner; or, as in Psalm 60, God is for me/God is against me. It is so much more difficult to live happily in the middle of these statements, bearing the uncertainty involved in being a mortal human being.

At the end of Psalm 60 the singer declares that 'human help is worthless'. This is a significant shift in understanding. We find that our normal ways of responding do not serve us well and we come to the end of our human resources. Neither reaching for the heights nor falling into the depths are going to take us where we need to go. We need to give up the extremes, to let go, submit, surrender and throw in the towel. This is a third way, and it is what staying on the train means. We can sometimes read this hard-won acceptance in the face of a person who is dying. There is nothing to push at any more, nothing more to be said and nothing more to be done.

Grounded in uncertainty

Paradoxically, it is when we let go, and accept the uncertainty of the journey, that we find ourselves standing on rock. This is a rich metaphor in the psalms:[1]

> Lead me to the rock
> that is higher than I. (Psalm 61.2b)

> The LORD is my rock, my fortress, and my deliverer,
> my God, my rock in whom I take refuge,
> my shield, and the horn of my salvation, my stronghold.
> (Psalm 18.2a)

God as a rock is an image of protection and security. When we have our feet on this ground we can *be* with our uncertainties in a different way. They are still there, but they no longer have the power to overwhelm us. Staying on the train means giving up control and staying with the uncertainty and confusion while the train travels on through all of the stations. The poet John Keats used the term 'negative capability' to express the potential of what seems at first glance to be death-dealing rather than life-giving. On 21 December 1817 he wrote a letter to his brothers, George and Thomas Keats, and in it he said this: 'I mean Negative Capability, that is, when a man is

---

1 William P. Brown, *Seeing the Psalms: A Theology of Metaphor*, Louisville, KY: Westminster John Knox Press, 2002, p. 19.

capable of being in uncertainties, mysteries, doubts, without any irritable reaching after fact and reason.'[2]

For those living with a life-limiting illness (and perhaps for us all) tiny steps and small, realistic goals will help now. This is very different from the previous fighting or despairing. A person is pushed in a wheelchair into the hospice garden to breathe in the fresh springtime air and look at the daffodils. A birthday or wedding anniversary is quietly celebrated, accompanied of course by cake. There is a trip back home for a few hours to say a final goodbye to a home and all that has been lived there.

We will respond to uncertainty in many different ways. There are times when we may be full of anxiety or panic; we may find the urge to organize things and people (the equivalent of cleaning out a cupboard when we are feeling stressed); we may find ourselves sinking into depression or despair, going to sleep and not wanting to wake up; we may become very 'religious' or lose faith altogether. The invitation though is to live the uncertainty. Can we go through this station to the next one? The desire is to run, but we need to stay.

2 Ou Li, *Keats and Negative Capability*, London: Continuum, 2009, p. 9.

2

Running Away, Needing to Stay

There is within me a deep desire to run from difficulty, darkness and death. From time to time I will see a job advertised, and I want to apply for it. This job (of course) will be far better for me than my current one. I want to run from this moment to a different moment, because I believe that the other moment must be better. And I wish to flee from the person I am to another person of my imagining (who cannot and will not exist). I want to leave difficult things behind me, because if I don't see them then they won't exist any more. From time to time I want to run from my soul-work sessions and so escape from the necessary journey where something in me needs to shift or die. I remember as a child hiding under the bedclothes because of the fear of a hospital appointment for my asthma. I would not come out. Let me hide, let me be safe, let me not face what I have to face. In my work in the hospice this frightened child can still make his presence felt. He wants to get away from death. He doesn't want me to be in a room where there is tension or distress, and he doesn't want me to ask difficult questions of people. He simply wants to go home and hide. My response to him must be very careful. If I ignore him completely or take too much notice of him, then his power and tyranny grows within me. I need to notice him, put my arms around him, listen to him, and then be quite firm with him! I can stay and discover the worth and strength of staying. Staying means keeping my feet on the rock of God's love. It means learning the worth of befriending my fear, and discovering that when I look my fear in the eye something immediately changes. I will find that when I look behind me at what I want to leave behind I am wanting to dis-card something rather valuable. And I need to be gentle with myself when I run again, because I inevitably will. The difference is I know I'm running now, and so I can ask myself what's going on, and how I may stop running.

We need courage to stay with our journey through all the stations of life. We may not be convinced of the wisdom of staying on this train, which takes us to so many new and bewildering places. We are unsure that this way, which is supposed to bring us to spiritual life, will actually deliver something helpful for us. And when one of the stations involves intense suffering, we would prefer just to give up on the journey altogether. There may well be a strong instinct to flee, scarper, run, escape . . .

Our shadow selves

It is important that we understand the particular suffering involved in being ourselves. This means looking in particular at our 'shadow selves', which are those parts of ourselves that are unknown to us and we do not *wish* to know. In fact, we would much prefer to deny their existence. These selves are the dark, fearful, self-serving parts of us that are begging for our understanding and welcome. They are also the unknown selves locked away in an inner cupboard which might be quite interesting and full of energy if we were to let them out. We would love to get rid of these troublesome selves, but rather than killing them off, the spiritual task is to put our arms around them, and hug them; then we can hear what they have to say. And what they tell us is that we are human, not superhuman. They tell us we are not God, but that we need God. Psalm 104 describes many delightful creatures from the natural world, such us wild asses and goats. But we also meet the dreadful mythical sea monster Leviathan. This fearful creature symbolizes the dark depths of the waters where evil and death reside. He and God are usually enemies locked in battle (in Psalm 74 God is said to have 'crushed the heads of Leviathan'). In this psalm something different happens.

Yonder is the sea, great and wide,
  creeping things innumerable are there,
  living things both small and great.
There go the ships,
  and Leviathan that you formed to sport in it.
  (Psalm 104.25–26)

He becomes a frolicking playmate of God's! Staying on the train as it takes us on means befriending our inner Leviathan, who usually has the aspect of fear for us. We may fear so many things: the unknown track ahead, death of one sort or another, difference in others, our vulnerabilities or perhaps our power. How difficult but how necessary it is to befriend our fear. The instinct is to run:

And I say, 'O that I had wings like a dove!
  I would fly away and be at rest; truly,
  I would flee far away;
  I would lodge in the wilderness;
I would hurry to find a shelter for myself
  from the raging wind and tempest.' (Psalm 55.6–8)

Run!

Let us look at what is happening in this psalm. 'Horror over-whelms' the speaker (v. 5), who seems to be a person of power, perhaps the king. There is violence and upheaval in the city (v. 9), which is normally a place of civilization and safety. The psalmist faces a catastrophic situation in which evil seems to have the upper hand. But the worst part is that a companion he trusted has badly let him down. This is a person he worshipped with and most likely shared the depths of his soul with (vv. 13–14). I imagine that in a time of great stress he would turn to this friend for encouragement and strength. Now he is completely alone. And what is his response? He wants to fly away to a safe place in the desert. The Temple, which is the refuge he would normally go to, is not available to him, because he might find there the friend who has turned against him. Fighting your enemies is one thing. Dealing with a friend who has become your enemy is another (this is the particular agony of civil war).

The image of the dove

The singer longs for the wings of a dove. Let us explore this image and see where it takes us. It can be a strange but helpful exercise to ask ourselves 'What sort of animal am I today?' By doing so we can find ourselves in the moment. What is my internal image at this point of my journey? What qualities does that animal have? When the psalmist imagines himself as an animal, it is not unusual for him to choose the dove: for example, 'Do not deliver the soul of your dove to the wild animals' (Psalm 74.18–19). A dove is innocent, fragile, potential lunch for birds of prey and may be used as a sacrifice in the Temple. In Southwell Minster, Nottinghamshire, there is a triptych in the Airmen's Chapel painted in 1988 by Hamish Moyle of the Little Gidding Community.[1] It was inspired by Edith Sitwell's poem 'Still falls the rain'. When it is closed, there is a scene of beautiful English countryside. Open it up, and there is a very different picture showing a dead airman in a landscape full of puddles, curled up on the ground, with crows waiting to feast on his body. Impaled on the barbed wire, wings outstretched in crucifixion, there hangs a dying dove. This is the end of flight for both the airman and the dove of peace. In Psalm 55, this kind of vulnerability, together with a terrible fear of death and destruction, has penetrated the soul of the writer.

Why does the psalmist choose the image of a dove? In this crisis, he does not see himself as an eagle, lion or wild bull, which are images used elsewhere in the psalms. The dove is an image of fragility and powerlessness, which is surely his

---

1   View this image at www.flickr.com/photos/23974177@N00
/530519995

experience. But the image fits so well, because the dove has wings with which to fly far away, and this is the impulse of his heart. 'Get me out of here!' is his one plea. In the prayer room/chapel in the hospice there is a very beautiful stained-glass window created by the artist Vital Peeters (this is the image on the front cover of this book). At the top is the image of a bird, its wings beating in flight, and this is the only clear image in the middle of other more abstract shapes. I often wonder how this image speaks to those who are in the hospice. It might well say, 'Get me out of here! Let me not be dying.' Or, 'Let this dying not be happening to the person I love. Let me be somewhere else. Let it be all right again.'

There are going to be times for all of us when we pray for the wings of a dove to take us far, far away. We may be trapped in a job which does not give life, or caring for a child or adult with a profound disability. We may live with a mental health condition that is managed by medication, but will never be 'cured'. Or it may 'simply' be a question of living with ourselves, knowing intimately the wound we bear in our soul. The impulse is often to run. And, of course, running may be the best option, if we have that choice. There are times when we will need to change jobs, remove ourselves from an abusive and deeply damaging relationship or leave a particular form of ministry or service. Running may mean loving ourselves enough to believe that life could be different. And, of course, there will be times when we need to run away for a while, to retreat, in order to come back to a challenging situation refreshed and ready to take up the battle again.

Staying with it

There are times, however, when we need to stay on the train, embrace our fear and discover life in the staying. Psalm 11 also uses the image of the dove. Another time of crisis is described in which 'the wicked bend their bows and notch the arrow upon the string to shoot from the darkness at the true of heart'

(v. 2). The king's counsellors are advocating escape. They say to him, 'Flee like a dove to the mountains' (v. 1b NIV). And the king resists this advice. His response is to trust the God who has set his throne in both the holy Temple and in the heavens. He believes that this God will deliver rough justice in the form of coals of fire and sulphur on the wicked! Doubtless he is afraid. He will wonder whether he has been foolish to refuse the advice of his trusted advisors. But for good or ill he decides to stay and face what he needs to face.

A journey with cancer can mean travelling through many stations of diagnosis, radiotherapy, chemotherapy, with times in hospital and times at home. There may be days of feeling well and weeks of feeling terrible, times of laughter and hope and times of wanting to give up altogether. If the time comes when treatment options have been exhausted, this is inevitably challenging for all concerned. Staying with the new situation for the dying person and their family may be immensely hard, and it would be very natural to want to escape from this final stretch of track. They have travelled through each difficult station in turn, hoping that the end of the journey will be health and now they are told that the ultimate destination is going to be death.

However, there are often rich blessings on this part of the journey as well as intense emotional pain. Precious connections between friends and family can bring delight in the middle of suffering. Important, poignant, soul-wrenching conversations (or silences) take place. Alternatively, people have mundane, beautiful chats with each other. Astonishing and everyday memories are shared. And there is that important sense for the family of 'we did everything we could'.

Tom was an elderly man who did not want to come into the hospice. He saw it as the Death House, a dark place full of fear. But his elderly wife, Elsie, could care for him no longer, even with the help of carers coming in three times a day, and the treatment of Tom's symptoms needed re-evaluating. When I met Tom, he told me quite candidly, 'I'm not ready to die.' But after a short while Tom had settled in with us. He had not been able to have a bath for a long time and luxuriated in soaking in a deep bubble bath. Tom became very fond of one of the clinical nursing assistants and talked to her about his life in the army and his work as a farmer. It made his day when she was on duty. Tom and Elsie did not have children, but over the ten days when Tom was dying, his nephew and niece and many old friends came in to see him. Often laughter could be heard coming out of his room. In the evening Tom and Elsie would sit holding hands, and very simply they told each other of their love and the pain of parting. Tom was becoming more and more sleepy, and it was difficult to rouse him. But one day he said very softly to one of the doctors, 'I'm not afraid of dying now.' When she asked him if he wanted to say more about this, Tom said, 'It's my time to go.'

Staying rather than fleeing can bear its own special harvest. But going through the necessary stations will take all of our courage. As we sit on the train, we will look out of the window and become suddenly interested in the sight of cows in a field. We will go to sleep. We will listen to some beautiful music. And we will want to do anything but attend to our fear and our inner Leviathan. Let's face it, it is very hard to do this by ourselves. At some point, we may well need some skilled helper to come and sit alongside us. Their job is not to tell us how to do the journey, but simply to encourage us to stay on the train, because this is what they have learnt to do themselves. We won't get to our destination in the course of a wet weekend when we have nothing better to do. This is a journey involving many stations, many waiting rooms, many diversions down pretty branch lines and some boring extended delays. The only necessary thing is to get on the train and to stay on the train.

3

Finding the Way

I was on a silent, individually guided retreat on the edge of the Yorkshire Moors. On retreat I can sometimes become a little spiritually super-charged, and I can 'fly' upwards in an unreal way. I remember walking through a wood pondering the verse Thus says the LORD: Stand at the crossroads, and look, and ask for the ancient paths, where the good way lies; and walk in it, and find rest for your souls (Jeremiah 6.16). *As I followed a footpath through the wood, I was earnestly trying to find God's good way for my living. I decided to use this as an exercise in trust. I would commit my mind and soul to this verse, to a total dedication to God's way, and I would trust God to bring me out on the road where I needed to be. I kept following the path, repeating the verse to myself. And the footpath ended . . . at a barbed-wire fence, which I had to climb over. I then had to trudge uphill through a muddy field and then climb over another fence to gain the road I needed to be on! I think this was a fairly clear answer to my prayer. God is not to be used for my own self-serving journeys. I cannot own him, control him, or make him dance for me. I need to find his way, not something that is a thinly disguised path for ego to walk on.*

If it is true that we need courage to stay with our journey wherever it takes us, we need to be clear about which journey we are referring to. We can easily confuse our own self-aggrandizing journeys with the track that leads to life. In this chapter, we look at how we may find a path we can trust.

A lamp to my feet

In the psalms the metaphor of *the way* is used everywhere we look, and in the New Testament it is the earliest description of Christianity (Acts 9.2). This is a physical path on which we can travel safely on our life's journey, but it is also a moral and religious way. It is the path of righteousness on which we journey with God, towards God. And we are told to be careful not to stray from this path, and to beware of pits or traps on the way. In the longest of the psalms, 119, the way is described as the way of Torah, or Law:

> Your word is a lamp to my feet,
>   and a light to my path. (Psalm 119.105)

We can easily think of obedience to the Law as dull duty. But this psalm is full of the energy and delight that comes from walking on the right path. The Law is given so that we may be happy and flourish. Finding God's way means finding life:

> You show me the path of life.
>   In your presence there is fullness of joy;
>   in your right hand are pleasures for evermore. (Psalm 16.11)

God is there to help us on the path, for *the way* will not always be easy. But if we stumble, he will reach down like a caring parent and prevent us from coming to harm:

> Our steps are made firm by the LORD
>   when he delights in our way;
> though we stumble, we shall not fall headlong,
>   for the LORD holds us by the hand. (Psalm 37.23–24)

Yearning for God

Psalm 84 is a beautiful pilgrimage song which tells of a journey to the Temple, which was thought of as the place where a person could see God's face and be with him in the closest of relationships:

> How lovely is your dwelling place,
>   O LORD of hosts!
> My soul longs, indeed it faints
>   for the courts of the LORD;
> my heart and my flesh sing for joy
>   to the living God.
> Even the sparrow finds a home,
>   and the swallow a nest for herself,
>   where she may lay her young,
> at your altars . . .
> Happy are those whose strength is in you,
>   in whose heart are the highways to Zion.
> As they go through the valley of Baca
>   they make it a place of springs;
>   the early rain also covers it with pools.
> They go from strength to strength;
>   the God of gods will be seen in Zion. (Psalm 84.1–3a, 5–7)

The soul of the pilgrim is like the swallow, yearning to nest close to God in the Jerusalem Temple. Throughout Israel there were ancient pilgrim pathways, and these ways are 'mapped' on the hearts of the pilgrims. But the journey is long and hard. The valley of Baca is a dry, desert place where nothing grows. They must pass through it, and then the rain is released that the desert may bloom. The strength and courage needed for the arduous pilgrimage is found not within themselves but in God. And when the singer proclaims 'my soul longs . . . for the courts of the LORD', he does not mean 'my' in the sense of a separate self. That self is our modern creation. 'My' means the whole community of Israel. These pilgrims go to find their true home again in community and in the presence of their king, who represents all of them. The pilgrimage is worth all their effort, and they follow their desire to walk to the place where community is and where God's presence is. They do not choose this journey for their own spiritual growth. They go because God sets within their souls a yearning for him and draws them to himself. His one desire for them is life.

I did it my way

Today we can easily convince ourselves that *my way* is the only way there is; a surprising number of funerals close with Frank Sinatra proclaiming, 'I did it my way!' We can guarantee that someone on a baking, singing, sewing, recycling or learning-how-to-thatch-a-roof competition will say sooner or later, 'This has just been an incredible journey.' And, of course, we do not doubt it. It has been fascinating to watch someone growing in skill and confidence. But if it is all about *my journey* then we are only just at the beginning. We are a culture besotted with *my* personal growth, *my* spiritual journey, discovering *my* past and fulfilling *my* potential. And if *my* journey means that I depart from *your* journey, well that's just how it is. I will tell the machine at the railway station where I am going and the stations I choose to travel through. At the top of the ticket will be written my destination: Life. And the stations I will travel through may well read something like this: Material and Spiritual Prosperity, Psychological Well-Being, Physical Health, Happiness and Success. This is where I am going, and where I must go. Anything else would be unthinkably awful, especially death in its many forms. Anything else would mean the loss of control. Perhaps most of our fear boils down to this – that I will not be in charge of my living, that I will not be able to determine *my way*. We desire to be autonomous, and most of us have a horror of being dependent on others. We cannot imagine ourselves having a serious accident, a stroke or a heart attack. We cannot imagine ourselves destitute, ill, disabled or dying. We say, 'I must be in control of *my way* at all costs. It is *mine.*' When things go wrong many of us feel cheated out of our 'right' to a successful life. But the great paradox is that it is precisely at this banana skin moment that a bigger way can open up for us.

When we are trying to find the right track to travel on, we have to start with *my way*. It is the only place we can begin today. I need to reflect with my anger, my desire, my spirituality and my ego needs.

When I was a young minister, I wrote a song in which the first line proclaimed, 'I've been trying so hard to be a Spiritual Hero.' I wanted so badly to pursue my own private, spiritual heroism, and felt for a long time that I could do this by myself.

In a thousand different ways this is what we absorb from our culture. And even the Church, when it misses the central message of grace, is prey to this distortion of reality. As a young man I felt that the survival of nine Cornish chapels depended on me! A hero is one who thinks he can fight a dragon by himself. But we quickly find that we are defeated by the dragon, and that this defeat is necessary for our journey to continue. When the necessary suffering happens, we will need people around us who love us. This could be family, a work team, a community, a church, as well as someone who is a few steps ahead of us with whom we can talk about the dis-ease of our soul and the true way. Through this costly endeavour *my way* is put in a bigger frame. I am no longer trying to do it all by myself. Now I know that I share my path with others. This revelation is often joyous and breathtaking, for one of our deepest fears is alienation. It takes courage to admit we can't do this on our own, and it feels full of risk, but we know we are on the right track now. Of course, ego hates this shift, because the way forward involves looking loss and failure in the face, and ego's job is to keep functioning and to keep the show on the road. Ego will do everything it can to stop this journey and to bring us back on to the old familiar track. But ego does not need to be Lord.

From my way to *our* way

A hospice is a place where *my way* can easily, gloriously, turn into *our way*. A daughter of a patient told me recently about waiting with her unconscious mother through the night. In the dark hours, she went to make herself a cup of tea in the day-room. As she walked down the corridor, she noticed a patient in the adjoining room who was lying awake. She made tea for both of them, and they chatted. A relationship began to build in a remarkably short time, and they found comfort in their ongoing conversations.

Pete was someone who wanted to share his journey with us. He was a regular in day services and talked to many of us. Pete discovered he could paint, and with shaking hand and bold colours he would describe his desire for life. Many people bought these pictures, and he proudly took the proceeds along to the charity office. One day when he was talking to me in my office, he opened up his heart and talked very honestly to me. With some trepidation I put up a piece of paper on the back of my door and invited him to draw images to describe his life. He came back to this poster week after week and kept adding to it. Pete wanted me to show it to everyone, to explain his journey to them. At the centre of it was a series of stick figures walking to a golden light, which was his death. He wrote by these figures: 'under warmth' – 'on my way' – 'one more step' – 'almost there'– 'I don't want to go on my own, please be with me' – 'Free at last'. And I featured on the poster too, a praying figure in the corner (an interesting image for someone who did not think of himself as 'religious'). These were the stations Pete was travelling through, and he needed to share the journey with me and others in the hospice. I conducted Pete's funeral service and the ceremony for the burial of his ashes. Because of the way in which he was willing to share his thoughts and feelings with us, Pete's journey to his death and beyond became *our way*.

My way will only take us so far. In many of his writings Richard Rohr describes the image of the 'Cosmic Egg'. He invites us to imagine three 'domes' of meaning. The smallest of these is 'my story' (which the psalmist would find hard to recognize). This is the story of the private self. The second dome is larger and is 'our story', where connection and relationship is celebrated. And the third dome is by far the largest and incorporates the other two. It is 'The Story' and concerns that which always holds true. For our purposes we may think in a similar way of *my way, our way and the Way*.

The winding path

It is time to turn our attention to *the Way*. Jesus, according to John's Gospel, proclaims, 'I am the way, and the truth, and the life. No one comes to the Father except through me' (John 14.6). This verse has been a battleground for those who have different ways of approaching Scripture. Many have used this text to assert that salvation can be through Christ alone. It is very human to assert that *our way* is the only way. But this results in well-intentioned people attempting to bring everyone else into their group, with the result that their group is seen as superior to other groups. Religious conflict is the result.

There is another legitimate way of understanding *the Way*. Consider a path which winds through all faith traditions and continues rising up beyond them all. What if there was a true track which people of different faiths and different ways of making sense of life may recognize? As we have seen, the psalmist thinks of the Way as the way of Torah, finding life in obedience to the commandments of the Lord. Christians will find the Way in following Christ and his teachings in a pathway of love. A Muslim will find the Way through Islam, which is the total surrender of his or her life to Allah. But *the Way* incorporates and takes us up beyond all of these separate pathways. Perhaps the only way of describing it is through the image of life through death. This may sound like a very Christian understanding, but it does look as though this is the structure of reality itself. Our cells are continually dying and being renewed in our bodies, the seasons turn from winter to spring, stars are dying and being reborn, and religions talk consistently about a life beyond this life, albeit in different ways. I like the concept of spiritual dual citizenship. I am a follower of Christ, and I desire always to be one. But I am a citizen of another mysterious reality too. This is the non-dual reality we glimpse which is beyond this religion or that religion, for it is the unity of all that is. This unity embraces all wisdom and all truths.

The Way will find us

The Way will find us when our small paths end in cul-de-sacs and we find ourselves being taken on to a wider track. This happens particularly when we are faced with death, that great can-opener of the soul. I wonder if Pete glimpsed *the Way* in his non-religious way? He knew the frailty of his body and spirit, and I think he saw a path that led to golden light and glorious freedom. Finding *the Way* will mean losing *my way* and even *our way*. We will look around bewildered on the track, our familiar landmarks gone, and we will not know which way to go. It is then that *the Way* will find us. If we think we've found *the Way* by our own efforts, we can be pretty sure that it is not the true Way we have found. We may have been trying so hard to find it, putting all our heroic energies into the quest for year after year. But in the end we have to give up and be found. And then we can learn to 'trust the process', or trust the Spirit, which boils down to the same thing in the end. In the next chapter we will look further at how *the Way* finds us when life falls apart.

4

A New Orientation

Easy life

> Very truly, I tell you, unless a grain of wheat falls into the earth and dies, it remains just a single grain; but if it dies, it bears much fruit. (John 12.24)

These words of Christ have followed me around for many years now. When faith was rekindled in me as a teenager, I remember singing the song 'Now the green blade riseth', which is based on this verse, with joy and understanding. The verse expresses a true patterning. The grain of wheat, safe among other grains on the ear of corn, must fall and die if there is to be the hope of a new harvest. This is the way of Christ, expressed in his life, death and resurrection, and it is the way to life for us all. It is *the Way* and contains deep within it what we may call the myth of new life. In the story of the grain of wheat this myth is perfectly expressed. If the grain remains a solitary grain, refusing death, then it has no generative potential. It is just a grain of wheat and nothing more. It needs to fall into the warm mud and lie there, perhaps for a long while, until the grain cracks and a green shoot emerges. And let's be clear, death is not just what happens at the end of our living, but includes the many little 'deaths' on the way. These are the dark nights of the soul, our failures, the capitulation of ego and our surrender to life as it really is rather than life as we would like it to be.

M. Scott Peck begins his most famous book *The Road Less Travelled* with the line, 'Life is difficult.'[1] He wants to tell us right from the start that suffering is part of the deal. But we live in a culture where there is another powerful story which gets told and retold. This is the story of easy life. We are told that life should be comfortable, that we will succeed if we work hard, that our standard of living will get better, and that if we continue to consume what we need we will be happy. It has led to a sick people and a sick planet. This is the story promulgated by some politicians, and which is told ad nauseam in the commercials. Television advertising portrays the shining people we think we should be, and if we do not live up to this perfection then we can easily believe there is something wrong with us. The story of easy life has its Christian equivalent in 'the prosperity gospel'. This gospel offers health, wealth and happiness to those who follow Jesus (through giving attention to selected texts that advance the argument). But can this story help in the face of rape or the death of a baby or when a life-limiting illness is diagnosed? In a time of crisis we need to be found and embraced by a stronger, more hopeful story which takes death in its many forms absolutely seriously but refuses to see it as the end. The myth of new life is that story. Please understand what I mean by this. I am not using the word myth in its popular sense of 'lie'. A myth is true, gloriously true, but it is a truth that is bigger than historical and literal truth. It is a story that describes how things really are, and is not the belief of an individual but rather the faith of a community.

Walter Brueggemann[2] has built on the work of other psalm scholars to give us a helpful and elegant framework for understanding the psalms. He allows us to see in the psalms how the myth of new life 'works'. He shows us a true patterning in the surprising way in which life emerges for a community. The

---

1 M. Scott Peck, *The Road Less Travelled*, London: Arrow Books, (1978) 2006.

2 Walter Brueggemann, *The Message of the Psalms: A Theological Commentary*, Minneapolis, MN: Augsburg, 1984.

story of easy life fades like the morning mist when it is replaced with the challenging but grace-showered way of orientation, disorientation and new orientation.

Brueggemann identifies first of all psalms of 'orientation', which are songs that speak of the firm foundations of our known world. They speak of creation, of God's constancy, human well-being and the spiritual strength of the Torah. Another group of songs he calls psalms of 'disorientation'. These are the personal and communal laments, often neglected by the Church because of the level of pain and disintegration they express. And finally, he identifies psalms of 'new orientation'. In these hymns of praise and songs of thanksgiving we hear of trouble overcome. The original distress may not actually be named, but the song is a response to God's action in resolving that distress. There is an expression of overflowing joy for deliverance and deep gratitude for the solid ground on which the singer now stands. This new state of affairs cannot be explained in human terms because it is sheer grace. It is not a return to the old condition of stable orientation, the status quo, but rather it is a jump into God's future. In this scheme we see how the myth of new life works in practice. The Way is found through following a path that enters darkness and death, before a new morning breaks upon us.

Orientation

I am settled in my ways and have a pattern to my week. I know where I am in my living, what has gone before and what will come next. The home I live in is known to me and is comfortable; I can sit in the garden and feel safe. I am secure in my family relationships. My bicycle journey to the hospice is so well known that I do not have to think about it, for my bike takes me there by itself. And at work I know all the staff; I have my routines of emails and meetings, of visiting people in the day centre and on the ward; all this has become familiar to me over the years, and I know at last that I belong in this place. I know also where I am on my journey with God; I have

come a long way and I am confident in myself as a person of faith.
As I drink tea in the early morning and open up my heart, I know
I am held in a great mystery. God is my rock and the foundation of
my life; his presence is everything to me; he holds me and all beings
in life.

We human beings take the normal day for granted. We like
to know that our relationships are more or less stable, that
our finances are not desperately out of control and that our
body is functioning more or less normally. Psychologists call
this 'basic trust'. This is our known world in which everything
is as it should be: 'God's in his Heaven – All's right with the
world.'[3] And when this trusted, known world is gone, we may
well find ourselves longing for the normal day. In the hospice
we sometimes receive people on to the ward who have had
a fairly recent diagnosis of a life-limiting disease. They may
have been living with an undetected cancer for some while, and
the shock of the news that no radiotherapy or chemotherapy
will be possible is potentially overwhelming. I remember Geoff
coming to us and his wife telling me:

But he has always been such a strong man. He's a fireman.
He's run marathons. He's always been active doing DIY and
working in the garden. I can't bear to see him lying in bed
like this.

We realize the value of the normal day when it has gone. Then
we may long to be bored again by the humdrum ordinary life we
have lived. It may not have been a particularly spectacular life,
but it was the life we knew and have been attached to from the
moment of our birth. A hospice attempts to maintain as much
normality for people as possible. That's why we allow pets to
visit and have no specified visiting hours. It's why until recently

---

3 This well-known verse comes from *Pippa Passes*, a verse drama by
Robert Browning published in 1841.

in our hospice the nurses did not wear uniform. We try to create as much 'orientation' as possible.

Psalm 30 is a beautiful psalm and very helpfully shows us orientation, disorientation and new orientation in the space of a few verses. Here is orientation:

> As for me, I said in my prosperity,
>   'I shall never be moved.'
> By your favour, O LORD,
>   you had established me as a strong mountain. (Psalm 30.6–7a)

There is a little bit of smugness in this statement, isn't there! In the state of orientation we can all be rather self-satisfied. 'I'm OK, Jack', can easily become our natural position. If I have enough food to eat, it is hard to empathize with those who are starving. If my faith feels strong and I am aware of living in God's presence, then it is hard to empathize with those who are struggling with faith. The royal mountain, Zion, on which the Temple was built is a symbol of God's protection and presence with his people. The psalmist believes that 'nothing can go wrong' so long as the Lord looks over him. His world is as stable and rock-like as Zion itself.

There is in our post-Christian culture a very strong expectation that if I am good then good things will happen to me. A woman called Jane said to me recently in our day services:

> I think I've lived a good life. I know it's the question that everyone asks, but why should this happen to me? I do feel punished. And look at all the evil people out there. They never seem to get cancer, do they?

There is a deep expectation in many of us that if we live our lives in a 'good' way, then we should be rewarded by long life, health and prosperity, and if we live a 'bad' life we should be punished by a short life, illness and failure. Like the psalmist we feel we should be specially 'favoured' because of the sort of people we know ourselves to be. This is not a Christian view, of course. The Beatitudes, or Blessings, of Jesus tell us that mourning and persecutions are a necessary part of the Way. It is when we experience downward mobility that we are closest to seeing God and when we are truly blessed.

Disorientation

It seems I am living on another planet now. My precious equilibrium has gone, and I cannot find the ground on which to stand. My world has been turned upside down, for I have failed again. I am being unmade. I am filled up with death. I was cycling to work on my familiar path and came to a 'T' junction. I did not know which way to go, because both ways seemed unfamiliar: I was totally confused and filled with fear. At work I do not belong any more; I have no confidence when I meet patients and families; I believe I will 'get it wrong' in some way. All I am aware of is the pain and distress that I cannot fix. God seems to be a very long way away. I try to pray, but I have no sense of God's nearness.

The ego will fight tooth and nail to preserve the status quo of the stable time of orientation, and so will the Church for that matter. We desperately want to believe that 'things are all right really'. The dominant culture in the West relies on happy smiling consumers, who will continue to be happy smiling consumers. And yet the evidence of our time shows breakdown at the personal and communal levels, economic instability, horrific violent and sexual crimes, mistrust of institutions, people falling off the edge into mental dis-ease, homelessness, addictions, the breaking of relationships and constant questions about the state of our health service, the care of the elderly and the care of those with disabilities. We are in a mess.

Psalm 13 is a personal lament which describes a situation where there is something desperately wrong in the life of the singer, and this 'something' has to do with his relationship with

God. This is no-holds-barred speech. He 'says it is as it is'. The psalm appears to be a fight between lovers:

> How long, O LORD? Will you forget me forever?
>   How long will you hide your face from me?
> How long must I bear pain in my soul,
>   and have sorrow in my heart all day long?
> How long shall my enemy be exalted over me?
> Consider and answer me, O LORD my God!
>   Give light to my eyes, or I will sleep the sleep of death,
> and my enemy will say, 'I have prevailed';
>   my foes will rejoice because I am shaken.
> But I trusted in your steadfast love;
>   my heart shall rejoice in your salvation.
> I will sing to the LORD,
>   because he has dealt bountifully with me.

The psalms of lament often refer to bodily suffering. 'I am poured out like water, and all my bones are out of joint; my heart is like wax; it is melted within my breast . . . (Psalm 22.14). 'My heart is stricken and withered like grass; I am too wasted to eat my bread. Because of my loud groaning my bones cling to my skin' (Psalm 102.4–5). We are used to the things our body can do, and the fearful experience of many who come to the hospice is of a body that can no longer function well. This body, which has been such a faithful servant for so long, is breaking down, deteriorating and giving up. Perhaps suffering is always about loss of control. As we saw in Chapter 1, we don't do well with uncertainties. 'How long have I got?', asks many a patient. A wise doctor will talk about months, weeks or days rather than a precise period of time. 'What will it be like? How long will the cancer-enemy triumph over me?' And for the supporting family, life has an uncanny way of giving people several challenges at once. The family dog has to be 'put down'; a daughter is just beginning a new job in a city far away; a beloved uncle has just died.

Sometimes people will want to blame someone. Doctors are often the main target. 'If only the disease had been diagnosed earlier; if only the right treatments had been offered; if only it was not like this, and we could go back to how things were before.' Sometimes God is the target. 'Surely if God is God, then he could have done something, or he could have designed a better world where cancer, motor neurone disease and every other disgusting disease could not exist.' The psalms do not hold back from accusing God of letting his people down. Psalm 44 lays the blame for the nation's woes squarely with God:

> You have made us the taunt of our neighbours,
>   the derision and scorn of those around us.
> You have made us a byword among the nations,
>   a laughing-stock among the peoples.
> All day long my disgrace is before me,
>   and shame has covered my face. (vv. 13–15)

This honest expression of anger might be quite uncomfortable for us, if we are conditioned to believe 'everything is all right really'. Walter Brueggemann writes: 'I think that serious religious use of the lament psalms has been minimal because we have believed that faith does not mean to acknowledge and embrace negativity.'[4] We can be concerned that our honest doubts and expression of dark faith or abandonment will undermine God's sovereignty. We are not sure if 'we are allowed', which is an issue about conforming to authority. Yet it is no threat to a truly Christian faith to express darkness and the unravelling of life, because this faith talks of a crucified God. This is a God who can understand us and stands with us in our distress when our world is undone. In Psalm 30 the psalmist finds himself in a new dismaying world of anguish in which he can no longer 'see' God. The context is most likely one of illness. He has fallen off the rock of his known life and fears that he will die. But this does not stop him addressing

---

4 Brueggemann, *The Message of the Psalms*, p. 52.

God, and in the style typical of the lament psalm, he argues with God. If he were to die, what good would that do? God would have lost someone who could give him praise and glory:

> You hid your face;
>   I was dismayed.
> To you, O LORD, I cried,
>   and to the LORD I made supplication:
> 'What profit is there in my death,
>   if I go down to the Pit?
> Will the dust praise you?
>   Will it tell of your faithfulness?
> Hear, O LORD, and be gracious to me!
>   O LORD, be my helper!' (Psalm 30.7b–10)

New orientation

The time of new orientation is not 'business as usual'; it is not jumping back into the old familiar pond. I still sit in the garden in the early morning drinking tea, but now I appreciate the tea as gift – in fact each breath is gift; I hear the raucous cawing of the crows and that unholy noise is gift. I am alive and celebrate the gift of my aliveness. I know I have not rescued myself. I have been brought through to a new freedom which is not of my making. I remember many years ago, when I had been in hospital for a short while and my wife was driving me back home, the 'ordinary' sights of the countryside and the ride in the car filled me with great joy. In the hospice I will not have to 'push' my work forward any more. Why would I want to push when I have experienced the gracious touch of God? I can be open to each person I encounter. Life is busy and I encounter much distress, and death is always near. But death is no longer such a threat, because I know I have been touched with life. And I know I do not work alone. There are colleagues around me who will support me and help me when I get into trouble.

Psalm 30 expresses the gift of new life:

I will extol you, O LORD, for you have drawn me up,
   and did not let my foes rejoice over me.
O LORD my God, I cried to you for help,
   and you have healed me.
O LORD, you brought up my soul from Sheol,
   restored me to life from among those gone down to the Pit.
Sing praises to the LORD, O you his faithful ones,
   and give thanks to his holy name.
For his anger is but for a moment;
   his favour is for a lifetime.
Weeping may linger for the night,
   but joy comes with the morning. (vv. 1–5)

These words are sung from the new spacious place of healing
and liberation. The psalmist has been 'drawn up . . . healed . . .
restored'. The language is most definitely up! The purpose of
the psalm is to remember, because disorientation will surely
come again. The message is hopeful: 'this is what God can and
will do. He is the one who can bring us out of the pit of death.
Silence is impossible.' This is not a return to the old place of orientation. The psalmist can no longer be smug and self-satisfied
because of this experience. There is a new song to be sung.

Surprising as it may seem, new orientation is a common
occurrence in the hospice. This does not come about through
avoiding death, but by coming to a hard-won acceptance of
death. As we saw in Tom's story in Chapter 2, when someone
first comes to the hospice there is often huge anxiety. Although
many patients return home after symptoms have been con-
trolled, a hospice is still a fearful place. A family may have
been dreading this day, when death is looking them in the face.
But a person who is dying and her family may quickly relax
and be glad of the 'holding' that is offered. They can now look
at their family with true gratitude and love, and conversation
will turn to reviewing family life or will focus on the immediate day-to-day concerns of life in the hospice. There may still
be anxiety about the practicalities of dying, but the pressure is
off. There is nothing left to do, or to fight, or to achieve. The

disorientation of the long journey with disease is over now. She can be her true self now. It does not always happen, but when it does, it is beautiful to witness. A person can shine with inner beauty, even though their body is emaciated and full of disease. She falls gladly into God's arms. It is almost as though she is anticipating now the life beyond.

When Geoff came onto the ward, he was very anxious. He was not a very sociable person and preferred the door of his room to be shut. It took a long time for the nurses and doctors to build up a level of trust with him. Geoff had not led an out-wardly 'successful' life. He had drifted from one low-paid job to another and had been living on benefits for quite a while. He had no long-term relationships and little family. His sister was the one person in the world he seemed close to. When I first introduced myself to him, he made little eye-contact, and it was very difficult to strike up a conversation with him. Geoff was not a very likeable person! He was quite irritable and obviously unhappy about being in the hospice rather than at home. I confess I avoided visiting Geoff. I don't think this was a conscious decision, simply that other people drew me in more than Geoff. And then one day a nurse said that Geoff had been asking to see a chaplain. I was very surprised. I went to see him and was immediately struck by a difference in him. He was able to look at me for a few seconds now, before looking away, and there was something different about his face. Our faces always give us away. Geoff's face was no lon-ger closed and angry. There was a new openness about him. He told me, again to my surprise, that he held deep Christian beliefs and asked me if he could receive Holy Communion. As Geoff became more comfortable with the idea of his death, he became more like his true self. He was again a small boy, open to an exciting world unfolding around him. He was a plant budding in the springtime of his life. Geoff could still have days when he was grumbling and complaining to the nurses, but more and more he was turning into the loving person he was created to be. 'I feel great love towards everyone who comes into this room,' he told me a few days before he died. As he said it, his thin, yellowing face was shining.

We are now beginning to see what the Way, which we discussed in the previous chapter, really looks like. It finds us through the many different aspects of disorientation and is not a path we would naturally choose ourselves. If we could choose, we would most likely stay with orientation, comfort and an easy life every time. But the grace of new orientation is given out of disorientation, suffering, and through stumbling and falling. It is the pattern revealed in Christ who 'gave up' heaven to be as a servant among us, accepted death on a cross, and through death was lifted to new life in the glory of resurrection.[5]

We can now draw together the themes of these first four chapters. If we have the courage, we will stay with the uncertainties of our journey, embracing our fear, rather than running away. This is counter-intuitive, because everything in us tells us to escape from death in its many forms. But the true Way to life, which is so much bigger than *my way* or even *our way*, is *the Way*, which takes us out of our habitual patterns of orientation, through the many deaths of disorientation on to the gift of a new orientation where we can sing a genuinely new song. We can describe this as the myth of new life. This is precisely the journey of many who find themselves as patients or family members in a hospice. The next chapters will describe some of the different 'stations' on the Way. For you, some of the stations will doubtless have different names, but I hope that at least some of these stations will connect with the track your particular train is travelling on.

---

5 See Philippians 2.5–11.

5

Dancing Off the Edge

I suspect that most of us would like to discover a new ease and spaciousness in our living without the necessary journey. I would prefer to run away from disorientation rather than stay with it. I would much prefer to get on the train and go straight to my destination (with God's help, of course!) Perhaps for some it can happen like this. But as I listen to hurting people and as I seek to understand my own experience better, I find that the more common route to heaven is via some version of hell. The myth of new life means that we lose our life before we truly find it. We fall into the depths and find no firm ground to stand on, until we put our arms around this experience. 'The Pit', that beloved root metaphor of the psalmist, will have the aspect of doubt, exhaustion, loss of control over our living, failure, physical debilitation or confronting death in its various forms. I do not want to hear this: who wants to go through the various stations of disorientation?

The depths

Our necessary journey often feels like drowning. The watery depths in the Bible are a symbol of chaos, disorder and death. The fear of flooding was a very natural fear, for it could mean the destruction of vital crops and also entire communities. With the change in our weather patterns we are experiencing that fear in our own time and our own country. Our prayer is that the dangerous waters, instead of covering the earth, should return safely 'to the place that you appointed for them'

(Psalm 104.8). We want a stable, ordered world to live our lives in. Let us return to the picture of the stained-glass window on the front cover. I often sit facing this window as I pray my morning prayer. It is an abstract design, but, underneath the bird in flight, my imagination makes out a figure in the central section and a wave going over their head in a swirl of blue. I do not know if this was the intention of the artist, but to me it is a stark reminder about the experience of a hospice. There are waters of fear, pain and distress here which may overwhelm us all.

Psalm 69 begins in this way:

Save me, O God,
   for the waters have come up to my neck.
I sink in deep mire,
   where there is no foothold;
I have come into deep waters,
   and the flood sweeps over me. (vv.1–2)

This prayer of alienation may originally express the anguish of the Davidic king who is overwhelmed by trouble. Perhaps neighbouring nations have accused him of annexing their land (v. 4) as a way of engaging him in warfare. He is now out of his depth, isolated and without comfort. All he can do is to cry out to God for help. John Eaton suggests the first line might read, 'Save me, O God, for the waters come in up to my soul.'[1] Is not this our experience too, when we are at the end of our coping? Our very soul, the core of our inner being, seems to be drowning. We are no longer the people we thought we were; we have toppled off the stage where we thought we were performing so well, and people now taunt us and throw insults at us (vv. 20–21). Our enthusiasm, zeal and compulsive over-working is turned against us (v. 9). We are aware of our foolishness and mistakes (v. 5), and there is a dark and deep pit which opens its mouth to swallow us up (v. 16). This confined

---

1 John H. Eaton, *Psalms for Life*, London: SPCK, 2006, p. 176.

space is the exact opposite of the spacious place where we may live in God's freedom. The image of the pit might refer to a dungeon, cistern, cavern, or a place where prisoners might be kept overnight and then brought up in the morning. There is a record of the prophet Jeremiah's captivity in a cistern.[2] He is lowered down by his captors and in the bottom he sinks into mud. In Oscar Wilde's dark one-act play *Salome*, John the Baptist, referred to as Jokanaan, is kept in a cistern in Herod's palace. The pit is a symbol of darkness, confined soul-space and the absence of hope. It is also the gaping maw of the underworld, the place of the dead.

The psalm describes a broken person who has lost hope: 'Insults have broken my heart, so that I am in despair' (v. 20a). In this situation it would be customary for the broken man to be sustained by a 'comfort-meal' provided by his friends to enable him to wait for hope to dawn again.[3] But instead of a comfort meal he is fed poison, and to slake his thirst he is given vinegar. To him belongs a complete alienation. And his response is to call out from the depths of his soul, 'I am lowly and in pain; let your salvation, O God, protect me' (v. 29).

Breaking

Those of us who care for others do not wish to admit we can break ourselves. We are the capable ones, the ones who hold the keys to health, strength and power. But we *do* break, and there are three main ways in which we can dance off the edge of 'normal' life and work. The first is through an accumulation of distress and sadness from the external world of our caring, which combines with the strata of distress already in our souls. There is only so much we can take. The writer of Psalm 69 talks of the 'Zeal for your house' which has consumed him; there is a keen awareness of making mistakes, and of the constant

---

2 See Jeremiah 38.
3 John H. Eaton, *Psalms*, London: SCM Press, 1967, p. 176.

criticism, insults and hatred of those around him. This builds up over the years until it seems he is falling into a pit. John Sanford uses the language of burnout to describe this experience (fire is a very different image from water, but the end result is the same!). Our inner being is like a burnt-out building; we have been fighting on too many fronts at the same time, and we have no energy left. He describes burnout as

difficulty in sleeping; somatic complaints such as weight loss, lack of interest in food, and headaches and gastro-intestinal disturbances; a chronic tiredness of the sort that is not repaired by sleep or ordinary rest and only temporarily alleviated by vacations; low-grade, persistent depression and a nagging boredom.[4]

We can exist like this for some time, realizing that something is deeply wrong but having no energy to deal with the root cause. It is very hard for people who care for others to say, 'I can't do this any more.' We *have* to keep the show on the road. We *have* to care to the last drop of our blood. It is who we are.

The second way in which we can crash is through a traumatic event. If the first scenario is one in which there is a gradual build-up of stress, then the second is characterized by its speed and violence. Trauma literally means piercing, and a traumatic event is one which pierces us to the core. The way in which our soul is traumatized, as opposed to our body, is through our wound. So, if our wound is to do with shame associated with our sexuality, then the trauma will come through the portal of our sexuality. If our wound is about our desperate need for attention, then this will be the portal through which the trauma will enter our psyche. If many of the psalms come first from the experience of the Davidic king, then we may see traumatic events mirrored in them. The external event – flood, famine, war with neighbouring nations – suddenly and dramatically

---

4 John A. Sanford, *Ministry Burnout*, Ramsey NJ: Paulist Press, 1982, p. 1.

enters the soul of the king through the wound of his powerless-ness. He is overwhelmed by his inability to protect the people or be the king he should be, and the flood comes up to his neck. This can be turned around when the crisis is averted. In car-ing work, the trauma might come through our body. We may come to a full-stop because of a virus or an infection (what are we infected with – sadness, helplessness, despair . . .?), or per-haps a scan reveals something unwelcome growing in the body. And of course we can be traumatized through our own partic-ular wound. We might have a conversation that temporarily disables us, because we come face to face with shame or terror.

The third way in which we can dance off the edge is what we might describe as breakdown, which is an inability to function altogether. We cannot do our jobs safely and need time off. The invective in verses 22–30 of Psalm 69 is very informative:

> Pour out your indignation upon them,
>   and let your burning anger overtake them . . .
> Let them be blotted out of the book of the living;
>   let them not be enrolled among the righteous. (vv. 24, 28)

I suspect that what we have here is the language of projection. The writer places on his enemies the depths of his own experi-ence. 'You just feel what it's like to be me,' he says. If we turn around the curses, we understand the king's desperation. He cannot see, he is trapped, he is living in a desolate wilderness, he feels punished and a million miles from forgiveness. Above all, he does not believe his name is written in the 'book of the living'; he is a dead man. Breakdown feels like death. It happens when there is an accumulation of distress, successive traumatic events, and then a final straw which is the tipping agent from life into death. When I was at theological college, I undertook a placement with a church where the minister was so exhausted that he could no longer talk; all his words had gone. The final straw might be a loved one who leaves us, either by death or by packing their bags and moving on. Or it might be a moral, shame-full failure in which we lose the reputation we once had. And we might experience a psychotic breakdown, because our inner conflicts are so great that we need to escape from an unbearable reality into another sort of 'reality'.

When we tumble head over heels down an unfamiliar hillside it can be quite a shock. 'How did that happen?' we ask ourselves in a stunned voice. We are too used to living in 'normal' mode (which can of course be a rather unreal, driven existence). We establish our comforting grooves of behaviour and so deny the possibility of change, let alone death. When the stress builds up and starts sending frantic semaphore signals to our soul, instead of sitting up and taking notice, we can deliberately ignore the messages and pretend that there is nothing wrong. Occasionally, in the hospice we meet people who know they are dying and who need to pretend to themselves and their family that they are getting better. We each have our own special way of crashing. There is a rich variety of ways in which we can fall out of the embrace of the normal. And what is left for us, now that we are stripped of our assumptions, habits and ego-strength? When we have danced off the edge we find ourselves longing for the normal day, and there is nothing we can do but cry out to God.

A story

I worked very hard in establishing a pastoral team of volunteers in the hospice. It was my Big Project, but it lasted only two years. I started with such high hopes, believing that the training, supervision and operational procedures were as robust as they could be. But I had not anticipated the awful souring of human relationships that would happen. And I had to own my part, my failure to manage a complex situation rightly. In the course of a few weeks I went from a book launch where I was flying high in the clouds, to sitting opposite my line manager who was investigating two complaints against me. This of course is very biblical! Did not Jesus warn us that those who are exalted will be brought low, and those who are

humbled will be exalted?[5] The activities of the pastoral team were
suspended, and for many months I was going through the motions
at work, trying to keep my head above water. And then the decision
was reached to finally stop the work of the team for good. When we
are vulnerable, exhausted and feeling defeated, it doesn't take much
to push us over the edge. It is not necessary to go into details, but
for me there was what I thought was a final straw and then a final,
final straw. My critical self was telling me, 'You are a failure, a
complete failure.' One day I found myself sobbing in front of my line
manager. All she said with great compassion was, 'Bob, I'm really
sorry.' It was all she needed to say.

Where do we go from here?

There can be a feeling of relief when we have finally danced
off the edge. I remember saying to my line manager (when I
could speak again!), 'This isn't all bad, you know.' I had used
up so much energy in trying to avoid this situation, and now
the worst had happened. I had been anticipating this loss of
reputation for a long time and dreading it. When the worst
happens, we can find ourselves in a different place from the
one we had been expecting. Amid the pain there is a strange
freedom. There is nothing we have to prove, and nobody we
have to please. We are pared down to the essential person, in
contact with our bruised soul in a very direct way. Our feet are
standing on new ground, and although we are exhausted and
full of pain, we know that we have stumbled on a surprisingly
spacious place. The train has taken us to a station we did not
want to go to, but when we are there, truly there, the station
is not as bad as it could be. There is a high roof to keep off the
worst of the weather and even a few green plants managing to
grow in the thin soil. And most importantly there are fellow
travellers who look as dazed as we are.

---

5 Luke 18.14.

When we dance off the edge, it is so important to describe the experience in words, paint, music, movement, or any way available to us. We must use the gift of imagination, for our experience cries out for expression, and our imagination is a good friend to us. I wrote a psalm:

God, you are my God.
I cannot blame you
but I can call out to you from the depths.
I am weary in my bones and my soul,
I am exhausted, I've come to the end
of the rope.
I cannot.
I go upstairs to find a book
and do something else and come down without it.
I have energy – adrenalin flowing through
my exhausted system, to flee or to fight.
I wake early;
and I have failed –
I am not God.
I turn my anger in on myself –
my fault, my fault, if only, if only . . .
turn the clock back, make it not happen,
keep everything under control,
don't fail, don't be angry.
They turn against me like
ravening lions – their teeth, their teeth,
and I am wounded deep in the soul.
Again.
An opening of the wound that has been there from long ago –
a wound of love, a knife in the wound,
and I cannot run and I cannot fight
so I need to opt for the Third Way
which is the way of
self-forgiveness and the
final (well final for now)
capitulation of the ego.

I will praise you yet
my God and my friend
who holds me in
this place.

By expressing our pain, we begin to embrace it and accept where we are. There will doubtless be the desire to put the pain in a box and seal it with a double seal, for expressing our pain can feel like putting salt in our wound. It is the last thing we want to do. And yet there is another desire in us. We must understand. We must learn and grow through this, or it will all be such a waste. There is a hope that this narrow place will open up, indeed we know it is already opening up. We cannot go back, we can only put one foot in front of the other and see where we are led. And we have to be very, very gentle with ourselves.

In our brokenness we will need to find our own way to the healing resources which are always there for us. This may be an actual time of retreat in which we review, reframe and recover after a time of breaking. Or it may be an inner journey, using the information given to us by our unconscious in our dreams and fantasies. I typed the following with my eyes shut, allowing myself to go where fantasy took me:

I dance off the edge. At first it's quite fun. I am capering down a hillside. There are sheep that scatter in front of me and clumps of heather to jump over. It is windy but the sun is shining. Then I trip and begin to panic. Now I am going head over heels, sideways, upside down, crashing into small trees. And it is all very fast. At last I come to rest. I find I am in a desert. But instead of sand there is grey dust. I lie there battered and hurt. Nobody else is there, and the sun is hot. I feel very sorry for myself. How has this happened? Not so long ago I was dancing along so happily. I see smoke in the distance and crawl painfully towards it. Suddenly the sound of horse hoofs. I am lifted. Barely conscious now, but feeling movement. It jars my whole body. I have a sense of apprehension. Friend or foe? Further humiliations in store for me? But then I see what I always knew I would see. A wigwam and a fire. She gives me water. I cuddle up in soft skins and rugs. I am warm, and

I am safe. She is there. Her wrinkled face does not smile. But she tends my wounds. Her hands are expert and gentle. There is the sharpness of poured liquid and a stinging sensation, but then the coolness of cream. And I sleep in the womb without fear. I sleep for many days. I wake to drink soup and to look at the Woman who is bringing me back to life. She does not speak. But she is in tune with her actions and with the wind and the sun. She is a part of it. I envy this oneness. I know that I danced off the edge because I was not in balance. I had reached too high. I don't know how long I stayed there. It seemed like a long time but it may have been just a couple of days. Time became timeless in that place. At times the wind blew hard, but I knew I was safe. Then the day came for me to leave. I was sad. I didn't know how to thank the Woman. I had nothing to give her. Perhaps that is the point. There is nothing we can give in the face of grace. Nothing to prove. Nothing to do but to take the gift on. So I bowed low to her and she smiled for the first time as she handed me a leather water bottle and a pack of dried meat. Then I began the journey back home.

I think many of us find it hard to give ourselves the time we need to mend. We can return to work, telling ourselves that things will be different now. We will never let ourselves get this exhausted again, we say. We will be sensible people. But it is hard to keep the promises when we have lived all of our lives pushing and pushing, trying to prove something to somebody. Some of us will dance off the edge many times, until we truly learn something.

Resilience and praise

As we travel through the stations on our necessary journey, we find something changes. There is always the possibility of falling out of the train, or losing our ticket or finding we're on the wrong train. These possibilities will always be there. But as we stay with the journey we find we will be able to deal with these in a different way. In particular, we will find we are learning resilience and praise.

I have found that some people working in the hospice movement are tired of the word resilience, because it has been overworked, but I still find it a helpful word. Resilience comes about through the coming together of vulnerability, experience and grace. It is counter-intuitive to think of vulnerability as part of our resilience. But resilience is not the absence of all weakness and frailty. It is rather a situation in which our vulnerability is safely held and contained. When I am fearful and distressed in the hospice, it does not mean that I will work in a way that is not safe. I will only do that when my fear and distress are not understood, reflected upon and thereby held. Second, we gain experience through our internal understanding of our soul, gained through spiritual direction, soul work, or counselling or psychotherapy. We also gain experience by reflecting on our work in supervision and remembering how we have negotiated our way through challenging situations in the past. Our colleagues are also our teachers, and we learn much through the hard discipline of working in teams. The third component of resilience is grace. This is the experience of the God of surprises who opens a door when we didn't even see a door, and when we can find the delight of joy and laughter in the middle of exhaustion and defeat. Resilience is therefore not something we can finally create ourselves: 'I was weak, but now I have made myself strong.' Like the addict starting a 12-step programme, we have to acknowledge our dependency on a Higher Power.

Psalm 69 ends in a renewal of hope:

Let the oppressed see it and be glad;
    you who seek God, let your hearts revive . . .
For God will save Zion
    and rebuild the cities of Judah;
and his servants shall live there and possess it. (vv. 32, 35)

This points ahead to the new orientation. There is something new given which could not have been predicted. The king and his people are delivered. The rains come, the enemy armies are defeated, the flood abates, the plague leaves the people, or the poor are lifted up. And they are not back where they came from. This really is a new place created by God. Resilience means standing in the evil day[6] and waiting hopefully for life to be renewed. In temple rites this may well have been waiting for the light of dawn, the time of God's salvation, which is when we can sing a new song. Then comes the daytime when resilience is fulfilled in joy and thanksgiving. We have stood our ground. Now God lifts us up again and our mouths are full of praise.

6 Ephesians 6.13.

6

The Breaking of God

At particular times on the Way we will have to face spiritual
bleakness. There are no angels singing encouragement in the,
trees and the signposts to the oasis have been blanked out.
What we are seeking is to be found through travelling on yet
another dark track of disorientation. C. S. Lewis wrote this in
one of his notebooks after his wife died:

> Meanwhile where is God? This is one of the most disqui-
> eting symptoms. When you are happy, so happy that you
> are tempted to feel His claims upon you as an interruption,
> if you remember yourself and turn to Him with gratitude
> and praise, you will be – or so it feels – welcome with open
> arms. But go to Him when your need is desperate, when all
> other help is vain, and what do you find? A door slammed in
> your face, and a sound of bolting and double bolting on the
> inside. After that silence.[1]

These words are wrung from the depths of angry grief. What it
boils down to is, 'Can we trust God and life?' Can the myth of
new life be true? We don't know, when we are in the middle of the
journey. Like C. S. Lewis we cannot see. We can be so full of anger
and distress that we cannot receive anything at this time. But perhaps this is a necessary station to arrive at. Jesus says to us:

> 'Enter through the narrow gate; for the gate is wide and the
> road is easy that leads to destruction, and there are many

---

1 C. S. Lewis, *A Grief Observed*, London: Faber and Faber, 1961, p. 9.

who take it. For the gate is narrow and the road is hard that leads to life, and there are few who find it.' (Matthew 7.13–14)

We get things the wrong way round. We think that destruction lies on the narrow track; after all, this is what failure and loss of control *feel* like. Surely life is to be found on the broad road used by everybody, where we are in control of our lives and feel more or less comfortable (if a little bored). Although we say that we believe in the crucified and risen One, it is still hard for us to accept that life, light and love become visible only after journeying on the narrow track through the valley of the shadow of death, with its sheer, slimy walls.

In the end, of course, as I have said before, the narrow track chooses us, for we would never willingly choose it ourselves. Through the boringly mundane or tragic circumstances of our lives, through an immense tiredness of having to live with ourselves all the time, through failure or unbearable loss, we find ourselves going down the narrow track in spite of ourselves. It feels like travelling into the darkness, because that is exactly what it is. There will come a point when the lights in the carriage go out, and we cannot see where we are going; this is very frightening for us mortals who need to know too many things. And as we pass through the stations, there will come a point where we are going to lose God. There is no getting around this unfortunately. Only later, perhaps much later, will we discover that we have to lose God in order to find God.

Absence

Psalm 88 is not an easy psalm. It concerns someone who cries out to God expecting an answer, but instead of an answer there is silence. The speaker starts off confidently enough, trusting in the God of Israel (who always answers):

O LORD, God of my salvation,
  when, at night, I cry out in your presence,
let my prayer come before you;
  incline your ear to my cry. (vv. 1–2)

But as the poem progresses, and there is no answer, the speaker becomes more and more desperate. In his anger he accuses God of causing his immense suffering:

You have put me in the depths of the Pit,
  in the regions dark and deep.
Your wrath lies heavy upon me,
  and you overwhelm me with all your waves.
You have caused my companions to shun me;
  you have made me a thing of horror to them.
I am shut in so that I cannot escape;
  my eye grows dim through sorrow. (vv. 6–9a)

Still there is no answer. He is dying and it will soon be too late. He is going to be lost. And all he can do is to keep haranguing God. Still he keeps 'saying it as it is':

O LORD, why do you cast me off?
  Why do you hide your face from me?
Wretched and close to death from my youth up,
  I suffer your terrors; I am desperate. (vv. 14–15)

In this psalm the singer encounters a terrible absence. There is no longer an experience of life-giving communion with God:

Your wrath has swept over me;
  your dread assaults destroy me. (v.16)

In Walter Brueggemann's words, 'Nothing works. Nothing is changed. Nothing is resolved. All things deny life.'[2]

2 Walter Brueggemann, *The Message of the Psalms: A Theological Commentary*, Minneapolis, MN: Augsburg, 1984, p. 80.

In our lives there may well be times when we know the springtime of God. There is energy, connection with people, excitement and the flowing, life-giving sap of the Spirit. But there is also the wintertime, when the cold wind wraps itself around the branches of our soul and we are shaken to the core. It is an immense effort to reach out beyond ourselves. This is 'the night-time of the day-time', to use Joanna Tulloch's words in the poem we started this journey with. We grimly hold on to God. We pray to him, speak his name to others and try our best to serve him. But our soul is frozen; nothing can flow. And what if this winter becomes an ice age? Perhaps then we have to face the possibility that we have deceived ourselves all these years and there is no God.

God is dead

There may be times when, with Friedrich Nietzsche, we cry out that God has died. God breaks under the weight of the violence we mete out to one another, under devastating natural disasters and debilitating disease. He dies a thousand deaths in the torture chamber, the killing fields, the oncology ward and the hospice. It seems he no longer comes to our aid:

> Never shall I forget that night, the first night in the camp,
>   that turned my life into one long night seven times sealed.
> Never shall I forget that smoke.
> Never shall I forget the small faces of the children whose
>   bodies I saw turned into smoke under a silent sky
> Never shall I forget those flames that consumed my faith
>   forever.
> Never shall I forget that nocturnal silence that deprived me
>   for all eternity of the desire to live.
> Never shall I forget those moments that murdered my God
>   and my soul and turned my dreams to ashes.

Never shall I forget those things, even were I condemned to
live as long as God Himself.
Never.[3]

With these chilling words Elie Wiesel describes the loss of his
self-identity and a solid faith in God as he entered Auschwitz as
a teenager. Any discussion about a benevolent God must begin
here. Can God really have a future after Auschwitz?

I once listened to a patient in the hospice who was struggling with his experience of life. He had a once-strong body
which was no longer responding to treatment, and this loss
of control was very frightening for him. Very honestly he
told me of his childhood when he was treated cruelly by his
stepfather. He told me how he used to cry out to God for
help, but no help was forthcoming. The abuse continued. As
an adult he could no longer believe in God. I did not try to
convince him there was a God. In fact, I could think of nothing whatsoever to say to him. All I could do was to place
my hand on the shoulder of this strong man as he wept.
Perhaps he would have identified readily with the desperate
calling out to God in Psalm 88, which brings no answering
response.

Epicurus long ago gave all religious people a huge intellec-
tual problem in his famous 'trilemma' – a difficult choice from
three possibilities:

If God is unable to prevent evil, he is not omnipotent.

If God is not willing to prevent evil, he is not good.

If God is willing and able to prevent evil, then why is there
evil?

Perhaps we must be prepared to let God break and die, really
die. And then see what happens.

---

3 Elie Wiesel, *Night*, New York: Bantam, 1982, p. 32.

God habits

For years now I have cycled to the hospice. My journey takes me on the towpath alongside the River Isis, from Kennington on the outskirts of Oxford, to Donnington Bridge, where I go up the steep path to join the road above. I cross the road to the cycle path on the other side, sometimes waiting several minutes to find a gap in the traffic, and then continue my journey by road to work. The other day I cycled *under* Donnington Bridge, up the path *the other side of the road* and straight on to the cycle path. I was amazed that I had never thought of doing this before.

I have met many good people who have been brought up with the habit of faith in the life of a church and have left disappointed and hurt when something tragic has happened in their lives. The message they received was that faith is about being a good person, and if you try your best to be a good person, you will be rewarded with good things. God becomes Father Christmas. When bad things happen, this person is totally unprepared and feels deceived; the belief system crumbles and God breaks.

And those of us who have a more 'considered' faith can also jog along with our beliefs unthinkingly. Christians tend to mix with other Christians, and Muslims with other Muslims. It can be very hard to examine our core beliefs, not to say a little frightening. What might we be left with? But we cannot simply believe what the tradition tells us. We must open our eyes, explore and experience the reality of the world. But habits of thought are so comfortable. Church leaders have a vested interest in not allowing God to break. We wouldn't have a job, a pension, a house . . .! Better by far to keep feeding the habit.

Those of us who have faith need the courage now and again to look at the opposite possibility. We need to stare into the darkness of a random world in which we have to create our own meaning. (For those who do not have a religious belief, the invitation is to stare into the darkness of faith and the possibility of a God who holds all in life.)

This world is the product of chance. There is no God behind it or in it. We are on our own in the universe and need to get used to that fact. All we have is our own resources. This does not mean an abandonment of morality. It is possible to reach out to our sisters and brothers with compassion. Our religious experience is something we create for ourselves – some of us carry the necessary God gene, and religious experience is produced in a particular part of the brain developed for that expression. Faith can be explained by our biology. Our desire for 'God' is the ancient defence against the harshness of human existence. We create the fantasy of a God out there who can help us deal with our human dilemmas because we haven't grown up enough to take responsibility for our living. We are the only ones who can help ourselves. When we die, we really die. The idea of a life beyond this one flies in the face of all reason.

Some years ago I was playing the part of a child in a piece of improvised drama. To my surprise I found myself shouting out 'I hate God!' The vehemence of this outburst startled me. But perhaps it is not surprising that those of us who are constantly told we should love God should end up wanting to express the opposite. What happens when we imaginatively kill off God?

He shatters into many pieces. A pane of glass. It is not an easy breaking. It took a lot of courage to wield the hammer. And I feel guilty now as I survey the fragments of God lying all around the garage floor. I also feel powerful and the power frightens me a little. I feel very alone. There is no point. There is nothing to do or say. It really doesn't matter any more. I can think what I like, do what I like, become who I want to be. I take the dog collar from my pocket and cut it up. Liberation. The burden of God is cast off. I am free to be the person I need to be. Free to find my own way in

life without the vast burden of church and faith and God to carry
around with me like a dead body.

Will the true God please stand up?

When I reflect on the above passage I find I do not feel free. In
fact I feel as though what I have done is rather adolescent! It is
quite cathartic to kill off God. But what then? I discover nihilism, despair and a space where God used to be.[4]

It is time to return to Psalm 88. Walter Brueggemann suggests that there are two possible responses for Israel in the face
of God's absence. We can wait,[5] or we can keep on speaking.
Israel keeps on addressing God, for this is part of her identity, and we see this in the psalm. The speaker does not give
up calling out to God, accusing and pleading. Even in the
depths of despair, Israel must still go on speaking with God.
Brueggemann calls this 'doing with God'.[6]

In the new atheism and in our experience of God's absence
there lies an invitation. To keep 'doing with God', so that the
true God can be – for the God we believe in cannot be God.
This God is an image, a habit and a provisional idea. The true
God is always beyond our thoughts and our words. We are
bound to anthropomorphize God because our humanity is all
we have. In some way, crude or sophisticated, we will make
God like us. This is why the psalms can speak of God's face,
hands and voice. The true God is more than this.

One day in the hospice I became extremely irritated (and
hopefully did not show it too much!). I was involved in a conversation around a patient's bed with members of his family. With
the chaplain present the discussion turned to God. One was

---

4 To be fair to Nietzsche, in his writings he was not just expressing
nihilism. He wanted human beings to be free so that they could realize
their full potential.

5 We will examine the theme of waiting in Chapter 9.

6 Brueggemann, *The Message of the Psalms*, p. 80.

saying he believed in God, while another said she didn't. 'How could God allow this to happen?', asked the patient's sister. We were trading the word God with one another, and the conversation seemed unreal. I sensed there were unexamined pictures of God being expressed but did not know how to respond, especially as the person in the bed was silent. The picture I had of the God under discussion was of a person in the sky who is like us but only a lot bigger. This God rewards the good and sends them to heaven and punishes the wicked and sends them to hell. After all, this God is embedded in the western psyche. This is the God our secular society has rejected. And I wanted to say, 'I don't believe in the God you don't believe in either.'

My experience of God is that God is personal and relational. This is why I am drawn to the psalms, many of which are intimate conversations with Yahweh the God of Gods. This is how I instinctively operate. I talk to this God, argue with him, reach 'out' to him. As a feeling person I desire a feeling God. And I know that this relational approach can lead to a big God in the sky who is remarkably like me, except a lot bigger. But if God is the opposite of this – impersonal, the unchanging, unmoved god of the philosophers, or 'the ground of our being' or 'being' itself – I have nowhere to go. How can I relate to such a God as this? I can only try to let go of my version of God, so that God can be God.

When I start to explore the death of God, another thought quickly emerges. Perhaps we do not need to kill off God, because in Christian theology God has already died. Is not the crucifixion of Christ the breaking of God? Following the perverse side of our nature, which despises that which gives us life, God is destroyed by human beings. God is at our mercy, as a person with motor neurone disease is at the mercy of her carers for good or ill. God becomes useless as we are useless, broken as we are broken. And yet somehow he manages to peep out at us from behind the curtains on Easter Sunday, and gives us a shy little wave. 'Sorry,' he says, 'but you haven't quite managed to kill me off yet.' A new identification is needed. This is one in which human breaking and disorientation, summed up in the experience of being 'cut off' (Psalm 88.5b), becomes identified with the breaking of God.

In the hospice chapel/prayer room, people usually gather together on a Friday afternoon for a simple communion service. There is often conversation at the beginning – normal, beautiful human connection, and then we share bread and wine. These symbols can speak powerfully. The broken body and the flowing blood of Jesus make sense to people who know they are dying, and the ritual holds us all. Underneath the words there is an identification with a suffering God. We address God and he answers with his own wounds.

Around the year 1094, Abu Hamid al-Ghazzali had a breakdown. He had been made director of a prestigious mosque in Baghdad in order to defend orthodox Sunni doctrines, and was a powerful speaker. But, as today, there were different strands of spiritual tradition within Islam and each claimed the truth for themselves. Al-Ghazzali was a man who was not content with simple answers. He needed to *know*. He set himself the task of struggling with the truth until it yielded some blessing. But he found he could not verify objectively the truth claims of any of the Islamic religious traditions of his time. The failure of this endeavour led to a huge personal crisis. He could not swallow or eat, neither could he talk or give lectures. The doctors he consulted diagnosed a deep inner conflict which needed to be addressed. He lost his faith altogether and was filled with despair. Al-Ghazzali was looking into the jaws of hell. He resigned his position in academia and went to join the Sufis. Their mystical disciplines gave him what he needed. He no longer had to discover God by reason alone, but could rest in the experience of God and find healing for his soul. It is so easy for us to make God up. Al-Ghazzali had wished to create a God and a belief system that would make sense to his rational mind. With the Sufis he found something different. He found grace, healing and renewal. He found God becoming God to him.[7] Three hundred years later the author of *The Cloud of Unknowing* reminds us that God is only 'caught' by love and never by thinking.

---

7 Karen Armstrong, *A History of God*, London: Vintage Books, 1999, pp. 222 ff.

Remember

I have just been down to the river with the dog, and I saw, just for a few moments, the moonlight sparkling on the water. A purely natural occurrence, but also an experience of grace – a hint of transcendence. When I was a young teenager, my grandmother was close to death. I walked in my distress, and saw a tree as it truly was, full of spiritual life and energy; it was a tree but so much more than a tree. Was this a mild psychotic experience, or was I glimpsing the reality of God hidden in the natural order? Whatever it was, it remains a precious memory for me.

When Israel encountered God's absence, she had memory. In the face of dis-membering she would re-member, seeking *shalom*[8] again. Psalm 136 is a hymn of praise, spanning creation, the release from captivity in Egypt and into the Promised Land: 'It is he who remembered us in our low estate', sings the cantor; and the people sing back, 'for his steadfast love endures for ever' (v. 23).

When we experience God's absence, is it possible for us to remember, or to allow a trusted friend to remember for us? Can we remember springtime in winter? Experience, the interpretation of that experience and our remembering of that experience is all we have. You may wish to remind me that we also have reason, tradition and the Scriptures. But when push comes to shove it is our experience of this world that we rely on. When I was alone and experiencing profound alienation at the age of 17, I was suddenly filled with an immense love and sense of oneness with the universe. This can of course be interpreted in different ways. One could say that the part of my brain that is designed to have religious experiences kicked in, and I had an experience of God. But this is reductionist, and does not fit the totality of what happened. This experience of love and acceptance was not emotional, it was not induced by a

---

8 The word *shalom* means so much more than 'peace'. It is wholeness, connection and well-being for the whole community.

crowded church with fiery preacher and swaying people. And it did not move me into the unreal world of psychosis, rather into the very real world of trying to serve my sisters and brothers. This is a precious memory, which serves me today.

On not having the answers

For those of us involved in pastoral and caring work there is a tremendous freedom in not having to have the answers. We can be honest with people and say, 'I don't know. Can we explore this together?' We no longer need to force God into a conversation, or feel somewhere in our soul that we have to persuade people to believe in God. This is not our responsibility. What we do need to do is live a life in which we can always be open to a more real version of God. This means a radical surrender of our small ideas and not a little trust. We are happy to live with Keats' 'negative capability', knowing we can never have The Truth in this life. The poet Rilke puts it so well in these oft-quoted lines:

> . . . stay patient with all that is still unresolved in your own heart, to try to love the very *questions*, just as if they were locked-up rooms or as if they were books in an utterly unknown language. You ought not yet to be searching for answers, for you could not yet *live* them. What matters is to live everything. For just now, live the questions. Maybe you will little by little, almost without noticing, one distant day live your way into the answers.[9]

The narrow track we have been following in this chapter is a tortuous, winding one, and the station we have arrived at is a hard one. But if we are to find God, we must lose God, and

---

9 Rainer Maria Rilke, *Sonnets to Orpheus with Letters to a Young Poet*, trans. Stephen Cohn, Manchester: Carcanet, 2000, Letter 4, p. 184.

the journey from complacent faith to disorientation to a new orientation is a necessary one for many of us. Wendell Berry's poem 'To Know the Dark' may help us to keep going forwards:

> To go in the dark with a light is to know the light.
> To know the dark, go dark. Go without sight,
> and find that the dark, too, blooms and sings,
> and is traveled by dark feet and dark wings.[10]

The singer of Psalm 88 tells us that although we may rage at God, or doubt his very existence, we still need to keep on stubbornly addressing him, because somewhere at the bottom of the well of our lived experience he is there. In the concentration camps some Jewish people somehow continued to practise their religion. One day in Auschwitz, so the story goes, a group of Jews decided to put God on trial. He was accused of cruelty and the abandonment of his people. In the course of the trial they could find no excuse for his behaviour, and he was found guilty. He deserved death. The rabbi gave the verdict, and then told the assembled people that the trial had finished and that they should now gather for the evening prayers.[11]

---

10 Wendell Berry, *New Collected Poems*, Berkeley, CA: Counterpoint, 2013, p. 121.

11 Armstrong, *A History of God*, p. 441.

7

Facing the Enemy

Now and then I fall into the unwelcome arms of ancient hurts. It usually happens when I am tired, and I am juggling too many things in my soul, with my family and in my work. The words and attitudes of another person, which I perceive to be critical or hostile, can take up residence inside me. My body feels hot, especially my hands and face, and I want to run away. The voice of my critical self begins a cacophony of accusations: 'You've got it wrong. You are stupid. You've made life difficult for someone again!' It seems as though my critical self is trying to kill me off. And so the urgent need is to 'have a conversation' with this powerful reaction. God understands my soul, for the soul is his creation, and I need to allow something to happen in my soul. I cannot make something happen, for that never produces life, but I can allow a process to begin. I take myself off to somewhere by myself and 'lower' myself down, deep into my soul. And I seek out my critical self, the part of me that is always harsh towards the rest of me. He is a bully. I hear his voice and feel powerfully his negativity and death-dealing stance towards me. 'You should not have! You should not have!' is his only cry. And at the same time I tell myself that he is not the whole of me. This is the secret. He is not me, he is only part of me. He feels so big that he seems like the whole of me, and I feel overcome by shame. But this is a lie for he is not all-powerful. God within me comes to my aid. His voice is not very loud, so I have to listen carefully to hear him. But he speaks. And I let him put his arms around my hurting, shamed, criticized self. Something actually, positively changes in my soul. There is warmth and light and freedom. I can move again. And I can love myself again.

The stations we travel through in this chapter concern forgiving ourselves and forgiving others. Many of us find it hard to accept ourselves as we are. If only we could make ourselves forgive ourselves! We may know intellectually that we are loved by God and forgiven, and we know that we are being proud rather than humble in insisting on holding on to our failure, shame, weakness and sin ('God, I am so bad you can't possibly forgive me!'). And yet to let ourselves be loved and to let the train move us on to another station can seem almost impossible. Of course it is, so long as we keep trying to accept and love ourselves. All we can do is to give up this impossible task and beg God to send us his grace. This allows movement again, but there are usually many stations for us to travel through, for our habits of self-denigration are deep within us. Again and again we find that the critical self will stop us in our tracks and detail how we have failed. However, as the journey continues, we will recognize what is happening, and the conversation with the critical self will happen more quickly. Other parts of our self will stand up for us and tell the critical self that she or he is not telling the whole story.

Loving kindness

The writers of the psalms knew that, in spite of everything, they were in a life-giving relationship with God. They faced the power of their enemies; they thought at times they were on the edge of the pit of extinction; they feared God's anger if they turned away from him. And in spite of that, the ground they stood on was solid; theirs was a radical trust in God's steadfast, everlasting love. They were bound to God through a holy covenant, and God was bound to them. They called this strong covenant love *hesed*, and it is most commonly translated as 'loving kindness'. This was a bond as intimate as that between husband and wife. The psalms invite us to receive this love. In spite of everything we can be confident that God knows us, holds us, desires us and is on our side:

O LORD, you have searched me and known me.
You know when I sit down and when I rise up;
   you discern my thoughts from far away.
You search out my path and my lying down,
   and are acquainted with all my ways.
Even before a word is on my tongue,
   O LORD, you know it completely.
You hem me in, behind and before,
   and lay your hand upon me.
Such knowledge is too wonderful for me;
   it is so high that I cannot attain it. (Psalm 139.1–6)

Mother God

When we are told that God knows us, one of our immediate reactions may be apprehension. We have seen how all our ideas of God must remain provisional, and that our picture of God must die in order for God to be God. We may have all sorts of unhelpful, primitive mental pictures of God that lurk beneath our conscious thought. For example, God might be a silent watcher with a frown on his face. But in biblical terms, God's intimate knowledge of us is the same as his love. He knows our thoughts, actions and desires in the same way as a mother intuitively knows her toddler. She hears her first complete sentences, sees her first steps and perceives her fresh soul. Her knowledge of her child is full of wondering love (and yes, she knows her perversity too, and her all too human desire to control the immediate environment around her). This love of a mother and of Mother God is primary: 'You . . . are acquainted with all my ways' (v. 3b).

Our ways are not always terribly helpful ones, for ourselves or for others. In Chapter 3 we saw how *my way* does not lead us very far. We can go off on our own ego journeys, persuading ourselves and others that we are on paths of service, and then we are surprised when we meet a brick wall. Our journeys can be driven by our need to experience love, or risk, or the approval and applause of others. These can turn into our night journeys, and perhaps we have to make them and discover the inevitable cul-de-sacs in order to grow. Particularly painful are our ways of self-hatred; as we walk these paths we know only a coldness of heart and we blame ourselves for our failure and stupidity. We use language towards our already hurting self which we would never dream of using to another human being. We berate ourselves for getting it wrong again. But God knows where we walk. God is familiar with every winding soul-path of the day and the night, our winter tramps through the ice and snow and our joyful summer excursions. God is familiar with all of them and has seen it all before. When we get stuck at a station and cannot love ourselves, we may hear the gracious words: 'You . . . lay your hand on me.' (v. 5b).

Hands of blessing

The beautiful (and very anthropomorphic) image of the hand of God is a common one in the psalms. It always denotes his power and the strength of his response on behalf of his people:

> Rise up, O Lord; O God, lift up your hand;
>> do not forget the oppressed. (Psalm 10.12)

The hand of God, and especially the right hand, means favour, support in battle and protection. Sitting or standing at the right hand of a leader implies the highest honour:

> You have given me the shield of your salvation,
>> and your right hand has supported me; your help has made me great. (Psalm 18.35)

> My soul clings to you;
>> your right hand upholds me. (Psalm 63.8)

In Psalm 139 God's hand is laid upon our head in blessing. He knows us and, in a contradiction of our self-condemning critical thoughts, he says good things about us. He names us daughter or son. His hand upon us is a steadying hand in difficult times. We are given confidence when we have no confidence of our own, and strength when we have no strength. His hand upon us is a vote of confidence. 'I believe in you,' he whispers into our unbelieving ears.

Henri Nouwen, in his delightful book *The Return of the Prodigal Son*,[1] considers carefully the picture by Rembrandt of the same name, identifying himself with the characters of the younger son, the elder son and the father in turn. He notices that the hands of the father, resting on the back of the younger son in blessing, are different from each other. The left hand seems strong and muscular, applying some pressure, while the right hand seems to be laid gently on him. It would seem that Rembrandt has deliberately made the hands different, painting his own hand for the left hand of the father and the hand of a woman for the right.[2] When we receive God's blessing, we receive the nurturing, holding love of the feminine, which keeps us safe, and the strengthening, empowering love of the masculine, which sends us out into the world again.

> For it was you who formed my inward parts;
>   you knit me together in my mother's womb.
> I praise you, for I am fearfully and wonderfully made.
>   Wonderful are your works;
> that I know very well.
>   My frame was not hidden from you,
> when I was being made in secret,
>   intricately woven in the depths of the earth.
> Your eyes beheld my unformed substance.
> In your book were written

---

1 Henri J. M. Nouwen, *The Return of the Prodigal Son*, London: Darton, Longman and Todd, 1994.

2 Nouwen, *The Return of the Prodigal Son*, pp. 98ff.

all the days that were formed for me,
when none of them as yet existed. (Psalm 139.13–16)

Gracious goodness

These words seem to describe the making of our physical being,
our body. However, the psalmist would not see a person as
we do, separated into body, mind and soul, rather as a unity
of being. These words mean the making of the whole person.
We are fragments of creation and as the creation is declared to
be good,[3] then so are we. Our innermost being is good, woven
like a sacred garment, and in the secret place we are given a
name that is known to God. The soul, the innermost part of
us, intuitively knows the God within who has made us. When
we experience the goodness of the soul, after a time of self-
criticism, this is life-giving for us; this is blessing, and a mirroring of God's loving thoughts towards us (Psalm 139.17). When
we cannot know the goodness of the soul, when we are 'against'
ourselves, completely stuck in our negative reactions towards
our self, it is reassuring to know that God is always for us.

Projections

Psalm 139 speaks to the souls of twenty-first-century people,
and it is very popular with many. But there is a section that we
often miss out when reading the psalm in public, and that we
must not ignore:

O that you would kill the wicked, O God,
    and that the bloodthirsty would depart from me –
those who speak of you maliciously,

---

3 Genesis 1.

and lift themselves up against you for evil!
Do I not hate those who hate you, O LORD?
   And do I not loathe those who rise up against you?
I hate them with perfect hatred;
   I count them my enemies. (Psalm 139.19–22)

Perhaps the singer is the anointed king in some kind of serious danger. He comes to God asking for help, hoping his thoughts and motives are pure, for then he believes God will come to his aid. He finds assurance in God's tangible presence. The king's hatred of his enemies could be seen in the context of his responsibility to protect his people. Even so, the words do not sit easily alongside an attitude of tolerance towards those who are different from us, and alongside Christ's insistence on loving the enemy. It is necessary for us to reframe the enemy.

We can easily project on to our 'enemies' the darkness we cannot live with inside ourselves. The popular media do this with patients at our high-security psychiatric hospitals and prisoners who have committed serious crimes. By describing people as 'monsters' we are all relieved from the onerous task of discovering and embracing the monsters within ourselves.

The enemy within

Another way of understanding this hatred of the enemy is to think of the enemy within us which we want to kill off. This inner Leviathan (who we met in Chapter 2) could be a weak, shame-filled, hurting part of the self. Alternatively, it could be a strong, sarcastic, critical part of us. If only we could be without this part of ourselves, we think we would be so much better off, and in a better position to serve others! If we were free of this part of ourselves, we could love and accept ourselves so much more easily! But the inner enemy is the one who desperately needs loving and accepting, and is the part of the self who enables us to have empathy with the hurting self in others.

C. G. Jung asks us:

> What if I should discover that the least amongst them all, the poorest of all the beggars, the most impudent of the offenders, the very enemy himself – that these are within me, and that I myself stand in need of the alms of my own kindness – that I myself am the enemy who must be loved – what then?[4]

What then, indeed! When we secretly wish to exclude part of our self from ourselves we come to a complete halt. The train cannot leave the station. It is truly humbling to be this poor, this incapacitated, this un-free. And it is so frustrating that we cannot just get rid of the troublesome, weak, shameful part of ourselves and move on by our own will and effort. We need to capitulate and reach out empty hands to receive something. And of course (damn it!) after the experience of the inner divine embrace, and our own gentleness towards our hurting self, something flows again. The train is off to the next station.

As we forgive

And what of the necessary discipline of forgiving others? Our relationships with those we rub shoulders with each day are the litmus paper for our spiritual journey as a whole. Perhaps most of the time we jog along with those around us, communicating well and not so well, but also now and then putting our foot in it and hurting others, or we might be bruised by another's words or actions.

In the hospice ward it is not just one person who comes to us, but a person in relationship or out of relationship with many others. Families can come together graciously when someone is dying, or the existing fractures can become even worse. There can be reconciliation between family members or open warfare.

---

4 C. G. Jung, *Modern Man in Search of a Soul*, London and Henley: Routledge and Kegan Paul (1933) 1976, p. 272.

Oliver and Sheila had been divorced for 12 years and had two adult children; they still kept in touch with one another. When Oliver was diagnosed with an inoperable cancer, Sheila took him to his hospital appointments and eventually looked after him in his own flat. She was very relieved when he was admitted to the hospice because she had become exhausted. Sheila had been caring for him out of a sense of duty, and for the sake of the marriage which had once been fulfilling. When we asked her how she was, she would say, 'My feelings are all jumbled up.' Sheila found she could care for Oliver in a loving way, and in response to his vulnerability she found a new tenderness towards him. At the same time she still found it hard to forgive him for his gambling addiction and his 'self-ishness' in regard to Sheila and her children. When he died she said she did not know quite how to react.

Our prayer for others will reveal those we find it hard to love and forgive. In our praying we will put up resistances and experience an unwillingness to picture them properly in our minds. There is no inner desire to reach out lovingly to them, and this is why we cannot prayerfully imagine them. These people are often very close to us. They may be family members, friends, colleagues or belong to the same church or organization as ourselves. It may be much easier to pray for those suffering in countries far away than it is to pray for the person we have to relate to each day.

Forgiveness as process

Often we are left trapped. We feel guilty that we do not forgive a certain person or even want to forgive them, and guilty that we have very strong reactions reverberating inside our soul. But guilt does not free us. Some teach that forgiveness is a one-off event. We are to gather our strength together and in one great spiritual exertion we . . . *forgive*. I no longer believe it is that easy. The first step out of our disorientation is not prayer but the safe expression of our resentment and anger.

I recently did a 'chair exercise' while I was by myself. I placed two chairs in my office, one facing away from the other. Then I selected two objects to represent myself and the person I was working with imaginatively, who I was struggling to forgive. I chose a postcard with the caption 'It's getting worse' to represent myself, and for the other person I chose a fur-trimmed glove. Then I spoke from my chair, my postcard in my hands, expressing honestly the anger and hurt that I was feeling. Next, I sat in the other chair, the glove in my hand and spoke as if I was the other person back to myself. Finally, I was able to move the chairs closer to each other and choose two different objects representing what I now saw. I chose a shell for myself, representing openness and contemplation, and a penny whistle for the other person, representing the creativity that I was beginning to see in her, which I had not been able to see before. When I met the person later that day 'in real life', I was able to respond warmly and positively to her.

A similar exercise involves writing down an imaginary conversation, and then to read it out loud. The key thing is not to shrink from expressing the negative and not to be 'nice' as we express it.

The process of forgiveness can take a long time, possibly a very long time. And when the hurt is very deep the closest we may get to forgiveness is the desire to desire to forgive! But a breakthrough can occur when there is a movement from the head to the soul. When our resentful thoughts towards another go around in our head, they are self-perpetuating; one thought feeds another, which feeds another. Having fully expressed our hurt safely, that is, without injuring the other person, we can sometimes allow the person to descend from the head into the soul. We should not force this, or we will do violence to ourselves. But there may come a time when we can offer the person our hospitality and receive them into our soul. They might feel very 'big' at first inside of us, perhaps quite vocal, but if we can sit with them, we may find we are given a new way of seeing them. We may find in particular that we can see their wounds and their fragility, whereas before we could only see their power, hatred or darkness.

These stations are difficult to stay with. We often want to be more powerful and more in charge of our life. Forgiveness entails giving up our futile attempts to change ourselves and others. We have to dust down our white flag of surrender, for we cannot forgive ourselves by ourselves, and we cannot forgive another by ourselves. It is always gift, the gift of a new orientation, and it usually takes a long time – much longer than we want. But, perhaps we can learn to allow something: the slow maturing of the fruits of love and forgiveness within us. And, who knows, we might actually come to like ourselves a bit more, and we might come to like other people a bit more!

8

Living our Death

There is an empty place in me that I must not fill up too quickly. It feels like the place of death. I stare into it, and it seems as though I am staring into the jaws of hell. It is hard to put into words. This place is so much a part of me that I do not see it clearly, and so I struggle to describe it. But the experience of being lost is on my skin and in my heart and soul. I cannot pray here with this absence. It feels like sickness and lethargy and guilt. I am not good, I am not worthy. I cannot give you anything from here. No wonder I am addicted to my life as I know it now. I am addicted to my own survival, and this is hardly surprising. I want to live long, and I have no desire to cast off my known life too lightly. The four Fs of Feeding, Fleeing, Fighting and Reproduction are all about keeping life going at all costs. This means it is extremely hard for me to hear the clear teaching of Jesus about losing my life in order to find it. Can I really open my clenched fist and give myself away? I'm not sure that I can die so easily. My ego would very much like things to continue as they are. And when it comes to my real dying, the actual ending of my life here on this blue planet, could I allow it, rather than grab and cling on? Facing my own death means facing the fear of my own annihilation, negation, the meaninglessness of my living, a total wipeout of life, goodness, love and relationship. No wonder I find myself working in a hospice. I am to stay here for a while longer, because I cannot avoid death here. I must stare at those fears. They are there right in front of my eyes. And I am gradually realizing that death is not the worst thing that can happen to me. The worst thing is to live a sort of half-life in which I am neither living nor dying, but trapped between the two.

Stopping at this station and staying with our fear of death is a hard thing to do, for death is to be avoided at all costs. This is the clear message of our western culture. If we are living the story of easy life, then what matters is how successful we are, how much money we have, how much pleasure we can pack into our days, how much power we can have over others, and how much we can consume. Death is weakness and the ultimate kind of failure. Consider the beauty business, which would persuade us to get rid of the 'appearance' of face wrinkles so that we can pretend we are still young. 'Don't get old and die,' say the advertisers, 'keep young, keep smiling with your perfect teeth, and keep consuming our products.' Look at the millions devoted to research on elongating life for a privileged few, when in many nations if a person reaches 40 years of age, having thus far avoided starvation, disease and a bullet in the head, they are doing really well.

Staring at our fear

The American psychiatrist Irvin Yalom has written a remarkable book called *Staring at the Sun*,[1] which is about facing our terror of death. I find the title very helpful. He uses some of Epicurus' ideas as a way of approaching the subject. Epicurus argued that because the soul is mortal and dies with us, then there is nothing to fear in a non-existent afterlife. When I am dead, there is no 'I' to worry with. And, in perfect symmetry, the state of non-being mirrors exactly our state before birth. Irvin Yalom acknowledges that ideas are not sufficient by themselves to dispel our inner fear of death, for living human connection is necessary too, often in the form of a therapeutic process. He discusses a number of people whom he

---

1   Irvin D. Yalom, *Staring at the Sun: Overcoming the Terror of Death*, San Francisco, CA: Jossey-Bass, 2008.

encountered in his clinical practice and the 'awakening experiences' that came about through facing their anxiety about death. Through uncovering their fear of dying they moved on to live much more whole lives. I don't happen to agree with Epicurus and Irvin Yalom about the mortality of the soul, but that is not the point. He invites us to stare at our fears, to stay with them rather than flee.

My shepherd

Psalm 23 is the best known of all the psalms today, and is still commonly used in funeral services, even when the religious beliefs of the person who has died are far from conventionally Christian. The words can speak to a grieving congregation with mysterious and hopeful power:

> The LORD is my shepherd, I shall not want.
>   He makes me lie down in green pastures;
> he leads me beside still waters;
>   he restores my soul.
> He leads me in right paths
>   for his name's sake.
> Even though I walk through the darkest valley,
>   I fear no evil;
> for you are with me;
>   your rod and your staff –
>   they comfort me.
> You prepare a table before me
>   in the presence of my enemies;
> you anoint my head with oil;
>   my cup overflows.
> Surely goodness and mercy shall follow me
>   all the days of my life,

and I shall dwell in the house of the LORD
  my whole life long. (Psalm 23)

Most likely this is a royal psalm spoken originally by
the king and is perhaps part of a ritual in which he is re-
consecrated.[2] The 'table' may refer to a communion
meal in the Temple shared by king and people, bind-
ing them together; God's shepherding and the shepherding of the people by the king are intertwined. The
confident personal pronoun 'my' fits well with the speech
of a king, who as representative speaks on behalf of all the
people. The king is the shepherd of the people, and they
can trust in his wise leadership, but God is the King of
them all. When the king says 'the Lord is *my* shepherd', he
says it for all. We have individualized this psalm, thinking only of *my way* through life, but it is more truly the
psalm of a whole community. The context of the shepherding is a rocky, inhospitable terrain. The shepherd
searches carefully for green pasture so that the sheep may
eat, and dams up a mountain stream so that they can drink
in the pool of water. The 'rod' is an iron-tipped club used
to defend the flock from wild animals, and the 'staff' is the
traditional shepherd's crook. The shepherd leads the
sheep through a narrow dark ravine, which is like
the valley of the shadow of death (to borrow the traditional language from the King James Version).
Death would wish to shepherd the flock into the
eternal dark, but God's desire for the sheep is life.

The hold on life is certainly strong in the psalms:

When the LORD restored the fortunes of Zion,
  we were like those who dream. (Psalm 126.1)

---

2 John Eaton, *Psalms for Life*, London: SPCK, 2006, pp. 55ff.

The survival of God's chosen people, the community of Israel, is of fundamental importance. Life means an ongoing connection with him in covenant love, and death was universally feared. The afterlife, *sheol*, was imagined as a grey place where the loveliness of life is gone for ever. The psalmist consistently cries against this fate, and I cannot find a psalm where death is welcomed:

'O my God,' I say, 'do not take me away
  at the midpoint of my life,
you whose years endure
  throughout all generations.' (Psalm 102.24)

Do not sweep me away with sinners,
  nor my life with the bloodthirsty. (Psalm 26.9)

For in death there is no remembrance of you;
  in Sheol who can give you praise? (Psalm 6.5)

I rather suspect that Psalm 23 is a psalm in which the king is wishing to avoid death. He leads his people through 'the darkest valley' in order to come out well and truly alive! His wish is to live with God in the closeness of his presence in the Temple, and death is a long way from his mind.

Our traditional interpretation of the psalm is therefore rather interesting. Certainly, at a funeral service, we understand that 'the valley of the shadow' is death itself. We go through this valley in order to find new life in heaven, however heaven is envisaged. Ironically, in a beautiful psalm that is actually about survival, we are enabled for once to contemplate our mortality and to look steadily at death. This psalm about life helps us to stare at death. I lead many funeral services for people who have died in the hospice. As Psalm 23 is read or sung, a congregation can find hope in the midst of grief. We can see in our mind's eye the Shepherd leading a person who has died, carefully and lovingly, through the fearful valley of death out and onwards to refreshing streams of living water. We can see that he is not alone in death, but that he is beautifully cared for and cherished. The biblical 'Do not be afraid!' echoes in our ears.

Facing the fear

Part of the work of a hospice chaplain (together with other members of the hospice team) is to enable people who are dying to look at their fears of death, if they wish to do so. People are afraid of different things. Many people do not fear actual death, so much as the process leading up to death. Because of medical advances and the hiding of death from public view, we live in times when we may come to our adult years without witnessing someone dying and without seeing a dead body. What is unknown becomes a magnet for our fear. We can fear dying in pain. And for someone with breathing problems there is a very natural fear of asphyxiation, of dying like a fish out of water. Some fear being confined in a coffin or being buried when they are not actually dead. And the fire of the crematorium furnace can have unhelpful associations with the fires of hell. The fear of what happens when we have died seems to be less common today, but for some there is a residual fear of punishment. Perhaps the most common fear is of being totally alone on the journey, separated from family and friends, travelling to an unknown destination.

Yet many people face these fears and are able to stare at death. When we are close to dying, I suspect it is very different from when we are viewing death from a considerable distance. Quite simply, grace comes to our aid, and in the great mystery that we face we know that we are not alone. When Jesus faced his fear of death in the Garden of Gethsemane something was transformed in the act of radical surrender: 'He said, "Abba, Father, for you all things are possible; remove this cup from me; yet, not what I want, but what you want"'(Mark 14.36). Jesus still hopes that the cup of defeat and suffering will be taken from him, but he intentionally reaches out for God's will rather than his own. Jesus leaves the garden under arrest, but something has changed within his soul. He and Abba, his Father, leave together.

What happens to the body as we die?

The dying that we witness in the hospice is usually peaceful. Most often, but not always, people will die pain-free. As people come very close to death they are usually in a very deep sleep and will not be able to wake from that sleep. Breathing normally settles down for those who have had great difficulties with breathing and often an oxygen mask is no longer necessary. Hearing and touch are the last senses to remain intact, so staff and families will keep speaking to the dying person, and it is a natural instinct to hold their hand. The colour of their skin usually changes, and their hands and feet become colder as the circulation becomes sluggish and the body begins to close down. Breathing will change. It can be noisy as mucus is not able to be cleared, and this is what is known commonly as the death rattle. It is horrible for those waiting and watching to hear, but so far as we know, it does not trouble the dying person. Breathing can stop for a while and then start up again, which can be distressing for those present as they may become convinced the person has died, only for the breathing to resume once more. Eventually breathing becomes more and more shallow, until it ceases altogether. This moment is usually very special and soul-full, for we are in that thin place between earth and heaven. It is also often a time of conflicting emotions for family and friends who are accompanying the dying person. There may be a mixture of deep, deep sorrow, a sense of terrible separation, and piercing joy, lightness, relief and tiredness.

The fear of dying

However, reaching the moment of death can be hard for some of us:

Mary was a woman in her early sixties who came to the hospice from the oncology ward. She was someone who had travelled the world with her business and had many friends supporting her faithfully. Mary was divorced, but her ex-husband David wished to be involved in her care and visited her frequently. Their daughter was at university in Newcastle but had come down and was staying now in the relatives' room in the hospice. Mary was very fearful of dying. Throughout her illness she had wanted all possible treatments and had been on a trial drug for a long time. The news that no further active treatments were possible came as a devastating blow to her. Coming to the hospice was a huge step for her, for it was the last place she wanted to come to. She had panic attacks in which she would struggle for breath and was convinced she would die in that moment. Mary wanted to have people with her all of the time, and to be distracted from her fears. She became very distressed if one of the team tried to ask her about the source of her fear, and we never found out exactly what she was afraid of. Our occupational therapist did some relaxation exercises with her; our music therapist took her to his amazing room and Mary made some music with him; one of the complementary therapists gave her regular massages on her feet. While these activities were going on, Mary would become calm. But when the person went away, her fears would return. Mary's family and friends did an amazing job, and they formed a rota, so that there would always be someone with her. They talked, they laughed, they shared meals together, and they remembered. As time went on, Mary slept more and more. This was a huge relief for those who were keeping vigil with her. Her anxiety was to a large extent taken away by medication now. Eventually she slept all of the time. Then, the day before she died, she suddenly opened her eyes and smiled broadly at the two friends who were with her at the time. She whispered 'Thank you' and went back into her deep sleep again. The next day she died very gently.

From tragedy to grace

Kathleen Dowling Singh is a transpersonal psychologist and psychotherapist, who has a great deal of experience in being with those who are dying. In her book *The Grace in Dying: How We are Transformed Spiritually as We Die*,[3] she explores a movement from tragedy to grace. Living with the reality of a life-limiting condition will seem like tragedy to most of us, but she observes many people moving from fear and distress to a serenity and peace that they did not expect to find. Her contention is that everyone who has a 'nearing death experience' knows the transforming power of grace, even if it is in the very last few moments of life. This is obviously hard to prove for everyone, but she gives many examples of those who are dying who move from intense fear to life-giving acceptance and trust.

I am sure that death is a radical discontinuity. It will be like the umbilical cord being cut once and for all. But at the same time I suspect there will be the familiarity of love, connection and light. We may even smell freshly baked bread just out of the oven and the aroma of freshly brewed coffee (please don't take me too literally!). It will surely feel like going home.

Life and death are one thing

Richard Rohr, in his non-dualistic teaching, suggests we have made life and death into two things, whereas they are in fact one. Dying we live. This is the myth of new life, which we explored earlier. The problem is that we become rather attached to our little

---

3 Kathleen Dowling Singh, *The Grace in Dying: How We are Transformed Spiritually as We Die*, San Francisco, CA: HarperSanFrancisco, 1998.

earthly lives. How would it be if we could see that our life is not ours at all, but that it's on loan for a period, and that when the time is right we can return it gladly to the Giver? We don't own our lives. That is such a very hard concept to grasp in the West where we own *everything*.

The only real answer to our fear of dying is to start practising dying now: 'Death is a stripping away of all that is not you. The secret of life is to "die before you die" – and find that there is no death.'[4]

Perhaps we all should have a skull sitting on our desk! This is an outrageous idea for us today, but our forebears knew that the way of dealing with death was to contemplate death. I am lucky, because working in a hospice I have to normalize death to keep on working here. I was once asked by a family to go and pray with their loved one in our viewing room, where someone is taken immediately after they have died. It was a very peaceful experience. I sat alone with the person who had died and offered prayer, and then I sat some more. As I sat, I felt completely at ease and realized it wouldn't be so bad to be dead!

Dying before we die

We *can* learn how 'to die before we die'. As I've mentioned, the cells of our bodies know how to do it, for they are constantly dying and renewing themselves. Perhaps we can learn from them. And the turn of the seasons means accepting the cold death of winter before the explosion of springtime. The rituals of so-called primitive societies show us how to die to childhood and become adults. Men in particular in western culture need to know how to do this so that they do not remain Peter Pans for ever. The ritual of marriage in front of the community means there is a once-and-for-all dying to the single life and an acceptance of the formidable responsibilities of child-rearing.

4 Eckhart Tolle, *The Power of Now*, London: Hodder and Stoughton (1999) 2005, p. 38.

Leaving school is a dying, as is leaving a job or moving house. The failure of a project or the death of a loved one (or even a beloved cat or dog) must be lived and experienced. And perhaps the biggest death to practise is the death of the ego. Ego is terrified of this death.

Let go

I have mentioned ego much already. Ego is not necessarily 'bad'. Ego wants to convince us that we are separate selves on our own private journey through life, and that we need to keep this important show on the road at all costs. Ego needs to feel in control of every situation and wants above everything else to keep things the same. Teamwork and accepting the assistance of others is very hard for ego, as ego wishes to do it all alone, unaided. The fall of the grain of wheat into the mud, where new life is possible, is anathema to our ego. Unfortunately, it is usually the case that ego only gives way to the necessary dying when suffering and loss is very great and when we have 'danced off the edge' in some way.

In the hospice, I have seen people die so slowly, and against all the odds they cling to life. Equally, I have seen people who can just let go into their dying. A patient may have just had enough – enough treatment, enough breathlessness, nausea, exhaustion, enough struggle. And she will say to me, 'I just want to die now.' She can look on death as a friend who will take her from this struggle to stay alive. I hope I can die like that, but of course when it comes to it I may still be grabbing and holding on 'for dear life'. I would wish, however, if I get the choice, to die willingly, embracing the adventure ahead. No short-cuts, simply living my dying. Tradition states that as St Francis lay dying he composed the last verse of his famous Canticle of the Sun, which refers to 'Sister Death', and his fellow friars sang joyfully the completed hymn. I would love to be able to welcome death gladly as a sister.

In the next three chapters, we find the train stopping at a station. The brakes squeal, the train slows and eventually comes to a halt. After a considerable amount of time it is clear that the train is not going to leave any time soon. There is nothing for it but to buy a cup of coffee and find the waiting room.

9

The Waiting Room

Waiting seems to be a defeat for my ego. While I can do something, I can feel I have some value. It is a huge relief in the hospice to be able to wet a dying person's lips with a little pink sponge, or to make someone a cup of tea, or to get on my bike and go off to buy cigarettes for someone who has run out (!) or to provide a prayerful ritual for a family when death has finally come to their loved one. I can become very enthusiastic about photocopying or going on a little walk to the Charity Office to borrow their guillotine for my compliment slips or deleting the many irrelevant emails on my computer, or creating a PowerPoint presentation. These things can fill the time, and settle me, and maintain the illusion that I am doing useful things. But what if the most useful thing I can do is to forego the ego's desire to be useful, with all the positive strokes that go with that, and just . . . wait?

The train stops . . . we get off . . . we go and sit in the waiting room. Many of us have stock phrases that come out now and then; they might be glib or they might be profound. One of mine is, 'Life is full of waiting, isn't it?' The world is full of waiting people – waiting with the beloved who is always in pain, for the results of a scan, with a parent who is aged and demented, or with a child who does not flourish. There are millions waiting for something to happen now – for a baby which has died in the womb to be induced, for food to arrive, for torture to end, for the flood waters to recede, for the funeral to come, for the day to be over, for the date of release from prison or secure psychiatric care to come at last . . .

A waiting that is not chosen

In the psalms waiting is described with stark, fearful imagery. When waiting is not chosen and the experience is one of stuckness and complete disorientation, the singer will cry out: 'You lay me in the dust of death' (Psalm 22.15b), and, 'I sink in deep mire, where there is no foothold . . . ' (Psalm 69.2a). This is a deathly waiting, waiting without hope; there is no nobility or dignity in this waiting. And the praise, when this waiting gives way to rescue, is intense. Some psalms express a more confident waiting. The singer of Psalm 57 tells us his enemies are like lions, that a net has been spread for his feet and a pit dug on the path he will take . . . *but* he has come through to safety: 'in the shadow of your wings I will take refuge, until the destroying storms pass by' (v. 1b). This is the new orientation which is always gift.

Loss of control

In the hospice, waiting can be very hard indeed. Giving up control, allowing the day to unfold and waiting on others for the care we need is very challenging for most of us. If we have always been in the driving seat in our work, life and relationships, then the loss of control involved in dying may be intolerable. Our body does not do what it has always done effortlessly. We may experience constipation, diarrhoea, pain, weight loss or nausea, and we are given what is euphemistically called 'personal care' by a stranger. Anxious thoughts can overwhelm us, or we might simply shut down and 'turn our face to the wall': better to close down completely than face this total humiliation. How difficult it is to abdicate control and wait peacefully for a death we do not wish to accept. And this can be just as much of a challenge for good religious people. When the chips are down it is hard to trust totally. And if we allow ourselves to rest in God and to wait with him, we are no longer in charge of

our very own spiritual journey! And yet, what if in the depths
of our distress we could call out to him:

> Out of the depths I cry to you, O LORD.
>   Lord, hear my voice!
> Let your ears be attentive
>   to the voice of my supplications!
> If you, O LORD, should mark iniquities,
>   Lord, who could stand?
> But there is forgiveness with you,
>   so that you may be revered.
> I wait for the LORD, my soul waits,
>   and in his word I hope;
> my soul waits for the Lord
>   more than those who watch for the morning,
>   more than those who watch for the morning.
> O Israel, hope in the LORD!
>   For with the LORD there is steadfast love,
>   and with him is great power to redeem.
> It is he who will redeem Israel
>   from all its iniquities. (Psalm 130)

From waiting to vigil

This psalm slows us down. It comes from an act of atonement
where the worshippers, perhaps praying silently together through
the night, can do nothing but wait on God for forgiveness and
the re-creation of their lives and their world.[1] The repeated 'more
than watchmen for the morning' has the effect of both calming
the soul and focusing the prayer to a single point of intent. This
is painful waiting from 'the depths' of the soul, but it is not passive waiting. It is a hopeful anticipation of the action of God. The
watchmen are waiting for the first light of the new day so that the
morning sacrifice can be made in the Temple, and the worshippers

---

1   John Eaton, *Psalms for Life*, London: SPCK, 2006, p. 334.

are waiting for the renewal of their community and the whole created order. We may properly describe this event as a vigil. Our word vigil comes from the Latin *vigilia*, a watch on the eve of a feast day. But it is interesting that the word is similar to the Latin *vigere*, to be vigorous, and the word *vegere*, to enliven. Certainly, in Psalm 130 we experience an event that is full of life and energy rather than soft and flabby. And this energy is given in our waiting. 'I wait for the Lord, my soul waits' (Psalm 130.5a). The Hebrew word that we translate as 'soul' is *Nepes* and means the breathed-into living human being. The psalmist is yearning for the time when the whole of our life is filled with the grace of the Life-giver. This can only come through our waiting.

Changing expectations

Some of the most difficult hospice journeys come about when someone is expected to die and they do not. Relatives have been called in because the nursing staff have seen changes and believe death to be imminent; they are good at interpreting these signs, but unfortunately human beings often do not die to plan. Those who are waiting nerve themselves for the final event, listening to each breath, watching for the signs of impending death. And, instead, the person gets slightly better. This unexpected gift of a little wedge of life can be absolutely wonderful, or, and this is difficult to admit, it might be devastating. Expectations do a handbrake turn, and another stretch of waiting is to be lived. Echoing the words of Psalm 13, the silent cry of the heart could well be, 'How long?' How long can this go on for – this constant up and down, this constant revising of expectations? We would prefer it if someone could tell us exactly how things are going to go. But sometimes anguished waiting can turn into vigil.[2] In the days and nights which follow each other without fail, where

---

2 I am grateful to my colleague Margaret Whipp for this insight about the movement from waiting to vigil.

there are no detectable signs of change in the condition of the dying person, something can settle. God is in the waiting, even if he is not named. Prayers are offered with the lighting of candles. A peace not of our making comes upon us.

This will not be for ever

Psalms 42 and 43, which are actually one psalm, express a time of suffering far away from the life-giving Temple. The psalmist is cut off from community. The experience is like a deer in a dry country longing for water, or, in a contrasting image, like being overwhelmed by flood water: 'all your waves and your billows have gone over me' (Psalm 42.7b). What an image of suffering! Many in the hospice would understand these words. Repeated through the two psalms are these lines, perhaps the first sung by a cantor and the second by the whole community:

> Why are you cast down, O my soul, and why are you disqui-eted within me?
> **Hope in God; for I shall again praise him, my help and my God.**

These are words that come from deep within the life of the community of faith. 'I shall *again* praise him.' We may not be able to praise God now, because we are cut off from all that is familiar and all we can do is wait. But, there will come a time that is different to this time. All things shall pass. This will not go on for ever. Sometimes waiting is hanging on by our fingertips. We want to run away, but we manage, just, to stay.

Waiting with

Sometimes in the hospice I believe the suffering is greater for the people who wait by the bed than it is for the person who occupies the bed. Simply staying there while your beloved is dying is an act of supreme courage. To wait with naked love when you would prefer to be anywhere else means digging deep. When I point out how courageous she is just to turn up each day, a relative will typically say, 'But I don't have a choice.' However, there is a choice, which she is making and continues to make. She could throw in the towel and board a plane heading for a sunny destination complete with pool-side drinks. Such escapism is rare (although one is allowed to fantasize about it). I remember a young man who was dying in the hospice some years ago. He had a twin brother who was a circus performer. On the day of his brother's death his twin spoke to me. He showed me his hands and said:

> These hands are capable of some amazing things. I can walk on my hands as easily as on my feet. I can juggle flaming torches with these hands. And I can stand on my hands on top of a stack of chairs, high in the air. But today these hands have done something even more remarkable. They held the hands of my brother as he died.

It's not all bad

It is remarkable how families do manage to stay with the waiting. Of course, people come and go. They have a day off, go home for a shower, or go out for a meal to experience a brief dose of normality. Often they talk about being in a protective bubble. The events of the outside world are going on all the time, but they are somehow detached from it all, curiously removed. And it is not all bad – far from it. Sometimes the waiting becomes a beautiful, precious time. Anxious expectation of the end of life can give way to loving companionship. This is always pure gift. Siblings who do not normally spend so much time together get to know each other again. There will often be the cathartic release of tears and laughter; under the pressure of this time tears can seem to be endless, but can suddenly turn into giggling and unrestrained hilarity. Family stories, often funny and occasionally unbearably sad, are told and retold. Love is expressed without embarrassment, gratitude for shared lives is proclaimed and requests made for forgiveness. This time of profound connection can perhaps give some comfort in the bleak months and years of bereavement to follow.

When someone is dying we are invited into the reality of the present moment. Everything slows down and the world becomes a small place. It is a terribly hard time, but if it can be experienced and lived rather than avoided and denied, this time can be a profound blessing. We touch the reality of *being* itself in this 'now'.

Staying in the now

In *From the Bottom of the Pond*, a delightful book on contemplation, Simon Small uses a telling phrase, 'the tug to the next moment'.[3] Most of us find it hard to be where we are. We will find ourselves pulled forwards from this moment to the dread or delightful anticipation of the future. It is so counter-cultural for us simply to wait. Thrusting, go-getting, successful, can-do people will find it difficult to wait. And yet by staying in the now we will see so much more.

When we learn to wait, we will find ourselves ultimately in a different place. This is a great paradox, is it not? It was when we seemed to be stuck for ever in the waiting room that, looking back, we can now see that we have moved. And we haven't done anything ourselves. We were powerless to move things on, but something has been done in us. The waiting of Christ in his passion, abandoned by God and his friends,

---

3 Simon Small, *From the Bottom of the Pond*, Winchester and New York: O Books, 2007, pp. 45ff.

takes him to resurrection. He couldn't do it; he had to let it be done to him.

Let it be

Embedded in the small book of Jonah is a psalm of new orientation. From inside the great fish Jonah prayed to the Lord his God. He said:

> 'I called to the LORD out of my distress,
>   and he answered me;
> out of the belly of Sheol I cried,
>   and you heard my voice.
> You cast me into the deep,
>   into the heart of the seas,
>   and the flood surrounded me;
> all your waves and your billows passed over me . . .
> As my life was ebbing away,
>   I remembered the LORD;
> and my prayer came to you,
>   into your holy temple.
> Those who worship vain idols
>   forsake their true loyalty.
> But I with the voice of thanksgiving
>   will sacrifice to you;
> what I have vowed I will pay.
>   Deliverance belongs to the LORD!'
> Then the LORD spoke to the fish, and it spewed Jonah out upon the dry land. (Jonah 2.2–3, 7–10)

This psalm is very positive, but Jonah, like most of us, had to learn the hard way about the worth of waiting. In the belly of a great fish, Jonah moves fast in the wrong direction, and there is nothing he can do about it. He can shout out his anger and fear, he can praise and give thanks, he can sit in despair, he can meditate serenely . . . it matters not! The fish will still take him he knows not where – and the end is not death but a birth. True, it cannot be very pleasant to be vomited on to an unknown shore, but most births are bloody and rarely as one would expect. True, it would be more seemly to be laid gently on the sand rather than vomited out together with seaweed and bits of half-digested fish. But transformation can feel a little violent.

The quick fix

Jesus talks about the sign of Jonah.[4] The people want a sign so badly. They want a quick-fix religion with a messiah who will solve all their problems, dispose of the Romans and bring in a new kingdom of peace and justice. Who would not want that? And they want Jesus to tell them that this is how it will be. But all he gives them is 'the sign of Jonah'. What sort of sign is that? It is a sign of true transformation. We look at Jesus and see his works, his death and resurrection, and we say 'how wonderful'– forgetting that this is our journey too. This is what following Christ means: to let the great fish suck us into its belly, to live in the dark and let transformation happen to us. It is the only way. We want to do it ourselves so badly . . . and we can't. The great fish comes in many forms and is never pleasant. She is our grief or shame or failure or helplessness. She dives deep with us in her belly. And this is where we call out and where we are heard, although it may not seem like it at the time. The shore we arrive on is different from the shore we left.

The sign of Jonah is the very opposite of quick-fix religion. It is like the difference between fast food and slow food; slow religion just tastes better. The way of the messiah is to go into the dark to suffer, to wait without power and to be raised on the third day. And this is our way too. In our

---

4 Matthew 12.39.

waiting we allow something. We give up being in charge of life. We give up happy endings and our fantasy of how we would like things to be. Reality can be hard, but it can also be a rock to stand on. We give up miracles so that we can live our relationships in the waiting – the miracles of shared memory and love and touch in the now. This waiting rarely feels 'good' because it is too full of pain. Yet there is a depth and a rightness about it too. Waiting is the final letting go of the quick-fix, the short-cut, the happy ending and the fantasy of the perfect. It is accepting how things really are.

10

Calmed and Quietened

After many years of pastoral ministry, I still find it hard to stop in order to seek stillness within my soul. This feels like abandoning the journey. I must be going somewhere. I must be on the move. The train will leave without me and will take the other passengers to some lovely places that I will never experience. Don't make me stop in another waiting room! I will be bored. I can't sit still. Let me do something! In the hospice, I will rush into a conversation with someone who needs my careful, considered listening and respond-ing. I will dash on to the ward, where I have no idea what I will encounter with patients, families and staff. Even as I am acting like this I know it is not wise. I know that if I were to open up my heart to God beforehand, the encounter would be so much more fruitful, because I would not be getting in the way so much. I know that if I can stop and seek stillness and quietness of soul with the God who gives life and energy through his Spirit, I will be the person I am meant to be. I may even find I am mirroring the stillness deep in the heart of God. I wonder if I could allow something in my soul? Perhaps I could listen to the sounds of the hospice around me, as I sit in the chapel; I could be aware of the cup of tea cradled in my hands; I could really see the candles flickering in their stand. Perhaps I could be aware of my breathing and even the beating of my heart. And as I try to be still my mind becomes distracted, and I start thinking about what I need to do. Perhaps I can give my hos-pitality to these thoughts and the anxious self which produces them, and then gently return to this moment in which I live and move and have my being.

The train stops again . . . and here is another waiting room. In our busy world, it is very hard to be counter-cultural and simply stop awhile. Perhaps we can have a little sleep. I know it doesn't sound particularly exciting, but there is great value in stopping from time to time. Then, because we have stopped, we can continue on our journey in a different way:

> O LORD, my heart is not lifted up,
>   my eyes are not raised too high;
> I do not occupy myself with things
>   too great and too marvellous for me.
> But I have calmed and quieted my soul,
>   like a weaned child with its mother;
>   my soul is like the weaned child that is with me.
> O Israel, hope in the LORD
>   from this time on and for evermore. (Psalm 131)

When this psalm was written, it was common for young children to continue to be breast fed until they were two or three. When weaning came, it could be a very distressing and frustrating time for the young child, who would naturally still be expecting the breast. We have in the psalm a picture of a child who has been coming to terms with this new state of affairs, peaceful after a time of struggle and agitation, asleep in her mother's arms. The singer of this psalm is able to help the assembly of worshippers to move from 'great matters', perhaps of prayers for the king, a good harvest or the safety of the nation, to a simple and complete trust in God.

Inner stillness

In our lives and work we may well spend time with great matters involving complex ethical judgements, sensitive pastoral situations, the political realities of the organization we work within, as well as the weighty issues of theodicy.[1] In this psalm we may hear a call, coming to us at just the right time, to move from the external challenging issue to a place of inner trust and stillness. This relationship of trust is pictured in the covenant between Israel and Yahweh, and describes how we may be with God and the people around us. In all our relating with others we need this quiet within us, for after a time of childlike trust and rest in the waiting room we can move back to the outer world refreshed and with renewed confidence and hope.

Drawn or driven

This sounds so sensible, and yet why do we find it so hard to put into practice? Our internal voices are one reason. They tell us, 'You've got to achieve something in this place', or, 'You haven't seen enough people today', or, 'You've got to do something here, this is desperate!' The voices are noisy and compelling and block out the gentle voice that is telling us to be still and wait. And these are not the voices of the Spirit. They come from our own personal drivenness and from a culture that wants to measure everything and applauds 'success'. No wonder it is hard to stop and be still, especially when everyone else is chasing their tail. Instead of blocking out the demanding voices, which is often an impossibility, we can choose to listen to them and receive the message they offer. They will always tell us something we need to hear. Only when we have given them our loving attention can we find stillness of heart. What we may discover is a child within us who is frightened of being told off for getting it wrong, or a starved feminine part of the self who longs to be more creative at work. Spending time with these inner selves is important. We can talk to them, paint them or play with the images they bring to our imagination. And

---

1 Theodicy is an attempt to make sense of God in a world where there is evil and suffering.

then we may find we are no longer struggling to *be* someone, to *do* something or to *change* how things are. We can allow ourselves to rest in God's embrace. One of our day services patients, a retired priest, was fond of quoting Corrie ten Boom who offers the words, 'Don't wrestle, nestle.' A calm mother is described in the psalm, and this calmness is transmitted to the infant in her arms. The masculine in us (in men and women) wants to strive for goals, targets and results. The feminine in us (in women and men) invites us to a relationship out of which something new may happen. But until we give ourselves to that relationship, we have no idea what that something will be.

Patience

Another reason why it is hard to stop and be still, is simply a lack of patience.

I tell myself that I have a lot of patience, but it's always good to examine these sorts of assumptions we have about ourselves. Although I hope I don't show it outwardly, I can be very impatient inside myself when someone is talking about what I consider to be trivialities, or when someone is repeating what I have heard many times before. And I can be very impatient with myself. When I lose the car keys or my reading glasses, I am anything but patient. I will give myself hell! In the hospice I find I sometimes just 'want to get on with it'. There is a fleeing element to this. If we get on with it, we do not have to think about our inner world and the pain involved in being where we are. It is often much easier to jump on a train than sit in a waiting room where all we have to do is . . . wait . . . with ourselves.

But, someone who is able to take the time to still their soul is someone who is able to sit easily and confidently within the organization in which they work. This organization, whether the Church or a secular employer like the NHS, will naturally demand our time and effectiveness. We are accountable to other human beings, as well as to God, in our work. But effective action grows out of times when we are receptive and open to the Spirit. I know I am more organized and get more things done when I am refreshed and in tune with myself and God. When we are stretched and exhausted, we find it hard to plan ahead, and we do not use our time well. We need reflection and times of prayer in order to perform our role. Stepping back during the day in order to recharge our spiritual batteries means we can do what we need to do. I was walking by the river the other day and saw a heron on the opposite bank, standing on a log, not moving a feather. Here is a stillness that will transform itself immediately into concentrated energy when a fish swims by. And this is the calm and quiet we need in our work. We wait in stillness, resting in God, and then take that loving energy with us into our activities. This can lead to an effectiveness that is as striking as the heron's rapid movement to spear the fish.

Into your hands

It *is* possible to be still . . . to stop and light a candle, or stroke a cat. It *is* possible to take a few minutes to venture outside to look at the sky and listen to the wind in the trees. When we do this we may well be aware of a pressure inside the soul, a guilt that tells us to 'keep on working'. We must listen to this voice and understand it, but we do not have to be led by it. We are not that important in the big scheme of things, and neither is our work. It can usually wait a few minutes. We can let the soul be, and let her become a soft child, asleep in her mother's arms. The words 'Into your hands I commit my spirit' come from Psalm 31.5 and were quoted by Jesus on the cross, according to Luke's Gospel.[2] They were the words used each night on going to sleep, an expression of complete trust in the God who stays with us

2 Luke 23.46.

through the dark. When we are caring for another we can learn to respond from this place of surrender and trust, knowing that our inner being is held in the Father's love.

Those who are dying can be our teachers in this:

Cameron was a man who came on to the hospice ward as he was coming to the end of his life. He had lived with a rare skin condition for most of his life. Now his skin was finally breaking down, no longer able to hold his body together. He was one of the calmest men I have ever met. When I asked him about his beliefs, or his ways of making sense of life, he told me, 'I'm like a canal boat, chugging along the canal. That's how I've always lived my life.' He quickly adapted to life in the hospice and seemed to be utterly content with his lot. Cameron never asked why this awful disease had happened to him, and to my knowledge he never railed against life or God. He was serene and genuinely happy to be with us for this last section of his canal journey. When his condition became very difficult indeed, the consultant talked to Cameron and his family about different ways forward, and they all agreed that sedation was the sensible option. Cameron died a week later, his canal boat finding its proper destination.

Refuge

In the psalms, God is seen as one who is always on hand to protect his people, deliver them from harm and give them refuge in times of storm and upheaval. The final words of the tumultuous Psalm 2 are 'happy are all who take refuge in him'. The hostile kingdoms can do all the raging they like against God and his intimate son, the king, but Zion will always be a refuge for those who are bound to God in covenant. Zion stands for a geographical entity but also an inner place of protection and safety. Today we might call it 'safe space' or 'sanctuary'.

A hospice has this function for many. I am constantly surprised by how many people refer to the peaceful nature of the hospice. I am aware of internal politics, tensions between staff members and the enormous weight of distress and suffering that presses down upon us. And I am aware of noise: the clattering of trolleys, the shutting of doors, loud voices and the sound of fast-moving shoes on the hard floor surfaces. I do not see the hospice as a peaceful place! But for many who come through our doors the hospice represents peace, safety, refuge and holding. A partner who has been caring for their loved one at home, perhaps having to persuade him to do things he doesn't really want to do, can now move back from the role of carer into the role of lover and companion again. There can also be a huge feeling of relief and security in knowing that skilled medical and nursing help is readily available, at the end of a buzzer. And this place of refuge has a spiritual as well as a physical dimension; it is that place where we know our soul is held securely.

Let us return to the metaphor of 'rock'. This rock is both a place to escape to and something solid to stand upon:

I love you, O LORD, my strength.
The LORD is my rock, my fortress, and my deliverer,
    my God, my rock in whom I take refuge,
    my shield, and the horn of my salvation,
    my stronghold. (Psalm 18.1–2)

The image of the horn of salvation comes from the four protrusions or horns on the altar in the Temple. These could be grasped by someone seeking sanctuary from their pursuers, and animal blood would be smeared on the horns in the offering of sacrifices. It is therefore an evocative image of security and holiness. The cumulative effect of the images in these two verses is very powerful. The repeated personal pronoun 'my' tells of an intimate relationship in which nothing can defeat the one who puts their trust in God.

The image of wings is another common way of describing this relationship. William Brown reminds us that Egyptian deities were pictured with wings.[3] In the temple of Osiris at Karnak, there was a statue of Isis with wings coming out of her hips, shielding her husband Osiris. In Israel the image of wings is a perfect metaphor for God's protective love in a time of external threat:

> Be merciful to me, O God, be merciful to me,
>   for in you my soul takes refuge;
> in the shadow of your wings I will take refuge,
>   until the destroying storms pass by. (Psalm 57.1)

The stopping place can be a place we escape to, as in Chapter 2, a fool's paradise where we are not facing what we need to face. Or it can be a place where our energies are renewed, a place of reflection and growth for the one who has weathered the storm and is able to rest on the other side of it. It is refuge and sanctuary. The waiting room on the station platform allows us the opportunity to breathe. It is all about different sorts of energy. There is a frantic energy which urges us to keep on moving, just to jump on the train and keep on travelling. And there is a different sort of energy, which we receive in quietness. This energy is life-giving; it always has the power of making things new.

---

3 William P. Brown, *Seeing the Psalms: A Theology of Metaphor*, Louisville, KY: Westminster John Knox Press, 2002, p. 20.

I I

Unless the Lord Builds the House

We have an open fire in our front room, and in the autumn and win-
ter time I love lighting it and watching the flames. I am fascinated by
the mystery of a fire that erupts out of 'nothing'. A fire requires wood,
and wood means saws and an axe. Sawing a piece of wood is a tricky
business, and if I use unnecessary force, the saw may well become
jammed in the wood, and I will huff and puff in frustration. A little
while back, I replaced the blade on our rip-saw and to my delight I
discovered that with the new blade all I had to do was move the saw
backwards and forwards, and it did the work for me! I have come
to realize I have two modes of working in the hospice. The first is
'pushing'. When I work in this mode, I think I have to do everything
by myself. I will move fast, but I am unfocused because my anxiety is
driving me. I am anxious about being perceived as a valuable mem-
ber of the hospice team, I am eager to see as many patients and fami-
lies as possible and oversensitive to people who do not wish to engage
with me. I also notice that I feel very responsible for the course of a
conversation and can easily ask too many questions and consequently
get in the way of the flow of the discourse. I can easily fall into con-
fusion and fear. In the second mode, I am deliberately 'going slow'.
I cannot do the work, for this is the mysterious work of the Spirit
of God. The outcome of a pastoral encounter is not in my hands. I
cannot make the Spirit dance for me. I am not in charge. And I must
remember that I cannot make myself arrive at the right place at the
right time in the hospice. When I try to do that I will surely end up
in the wrong place at the wrong time, feeling very foolish. I know I
need to pray. It may not be much prayer, but, aware of my anxiety, I
intentionally turn my soul to God's light, and ask for the help of his

Spirit. I move slowly and find that I am talking to people whom I hadn't anticipated meeting. I am peaceful in my soul and find myself enjoying the encounters I have with people, even though some of them may be challenging. I find to my surprise that people seem to trust me, and I can forget about myself and concentrate on what they are saying. I relax, because I am not responsible for the outcome of the conversation. I don't have to fix or change or console or offer hope. I am simply there.

> Unless the LORD builds the house,
>   those who build it labour in vain.
> Unless the LORD guards the city,
>   the guard keeps watch in vain.
> It is in vain that you rise up early
>   and go late to rest,
> eating the bread of anxious toil;
>   for he gives sleep to his beloved. (Psalm 127.1–3)

Many of us need to receive the teaching of this short psalm, for we live in a culture that overvalues self-sufficiency and where work can take over and become the sole reason for our living. The singer of the psalm says that it is all 'in vain'. There will be no lasting fruit from our frantic activity when we are pushing too hard or when we are trying to prove something to somebody by our efforts. One thing we can be certain of: we will never impress 'them' (boss, internalized parent, God) in the way we want. We need to allow God to build the house and to watch over the city. This does not mean doing nothing at all ourselves. It means the springs of our activity can change. Instead of our activities coming from the ego, they can bubble up from God's love within us. The psalmist says that when we are no longer 'pushing', we can be given something, through the unconscious as we sleep. The contrast is between a self-obsessed, anxious life and a life lived freely in the light of God's grace. The psalm goes on to talk about children as a gift of God:

Like arrows in the hand of a warrior
are the sons of one's youth. (Psalms 127.4)

All is gift

We may understand the biology involved in 'making' a child, but should never lose the sense of miracle when a child is born. In the time of the psalms, childlessness was not only shameful but could mean dire poverty in old age, because there would be none to give financial support. The psalmist points out that these children, in future years, could act as a defence team if legal action is taken. The message of the psalm is that all is gift, if we could but see it. The reference to sleep is interesting. Sleep is a time when we are completely passive, and something can be given to us. When a king sleeps, it is a dangerous time. This is when his enemies could attack and get the upper hand, so he must trust completely in God:

I lie down and sleep;
I wake again, for the LORD sustains me. (Psalm 3.5)

In the hospice sleep is the gift of the tired body. The body says *sleep*, and he or she sleeps. Just as a baby sleeps much at the beginning of life, so we tend to sleep at the end of life. And there are many other simple gifts on offer in the hospice: a cup of tea; a conversation with one of the housekeepers who is mopping under the bed; a joke with the nurses who come in to alter his position in the bed; the smell of a bouquet of flowers; a card from a relative who lives in New Zealand; the setting up of a syringe driver, that clever pump that delivers pain relief and other medication in small, regular doses; a bath in which he can let the water take all of his weight; a trip out in a wheelchair when he can feel the wind on his face and the heat of the sun on his skin. There are many gifts on offer in this challenging time.

And those of us who are 'staff' can receive gifts from those who are dying:

> Marjorie was a woman who in her dying touched many of us. She had had quite a tough life, losing her husband at an early age and bringing up four children by herself. Two of her children had subsequently died. She had always worked as a school 'dinner lady' and was loved by many generations of children. And now she was facing her death. Now and then we meet someone who is 'good' to the core of their being. They are always more concerned about those who are looking after them than about themselves, and they are profoundly grateful for the help they are receiving. Perhaps it is worth saying that they are not always religious people. Marjorie was one such delightful human being. The nursing team fought over who would look after her, and when one of them was off for a few days, she would make a point of coming to see Marjorie and saying goodbye to her before she left. I did not have many profound conversations with Marjorie, but I certainly enjoyed being with her. I would sit with her, holding her hand, not needing to do much except concentrate on being as present as I could in the moment. Occasionally she would open her large, brown eyes and look at me. It was as though you could see right through them into her soul. When Marjorie died, we all felt glad that we had known her, for she had given us so much.

Work as grace

If life is gift, and if in dying there can be gift, then what of our work? If we could see our work as God's grace working in us, rather than as our own achievement, I think we might be happier people! Psalm 104, that great psalm of creation, advocates an 'ecocentric' rather than an 'anthropocentric' view of the world.[1] Animals and birds, plants and trees are wondered over, but for the first 13 verses there is no mention of people at all! When the psalmist asserts, 'These all look to you to give them their food in due season (v. 27), he means animals and human beings together. And there is a different way of looking at our work: 'People go out to their work and to their labour until the evening.' This is not work as punishment or anxious toiling, but work as part of the natural order of things. At night-time the wild animals work the night shift, 'seeking their food from God' (v. 21b) and then human beings take over for the day shift. This is how it is meant to be under God's loving kindness.

The further journey

Richard Rohr, in his beautiful book *Falling Upwards*,[2] follows Dr Jung in distinguishing between the two halves of life. In the first half we are creating a container, and in the second half we are discovering the contents with which to fill that container. The first half is about working to establish our identity and making a mark on the world. This is the right time to 'build the house' ourselves. We need to establish our identity, create boundaries and push against them, find some ego strength and good power for ourselves. This is the time of life when we can be confident of our place in the world. We need a few achievements to ground ourselves and become confident in this person we are becoming. The second half of life begins with necessary suffering, a surrender of ego, a fall, and involves a 'further journey' (as Odysseus in the *Iliad*) of the soul into mystery and a much bigger life where we are no longer in control of our destiny. We can no longer work to make this happen. It has to be

1   William P. Brown, *Seeing the Psalms: A Theology of Metaphor*, Louisville, KY: Westminster John Knox Press, 2002, pp. 158ff.

2   Richard Rohr, *Falling Upwards: A Spirituality for the Two Halves of Life*, San Francisco, CA: Jossey-Bass, 2011.

given and received. What was appropriate once will no longer be so. C. G. Jung says:

> One cannot live the afternoon of life according to the pro-gramme of life's morning, for what was great in the morning will be of little importance in the evening, and what in the morning was true will at evening have become a lie.[3]

In the stories about Elijah in 1 Kings 18–19 the prophet is in 'first half' of life mode when he battles with the prophets of Baal on Mount Carmel; he and God win a famous victory between them. The painful transition to another kind of life happens when he flees from Jezebel, running from his fear into the wilderness, and wishing for death. He believes it's all over. In spite of the victory, the religion of God now seems to be extinguished in the land, and he thinks he is the only true believer left. The 'second half' encounter is on a different mountain, Mount Hermon, when his soul is awakened by a still small voice. A new perspective opens up for him in which Elijah the prophet is now just a bit-player in a much bigger salvation drama. He discovers he is not alone, indeed there are seven thousand people who still remain loyal to the faith. True kings are to be anointed and a trainee prophet to be recruited who will take up the fight after him. He does not have to try quite so hard, for God has got there before him!

No short cuts

In the second half of life we realize that life is not just about us. Most of us want to stay in the first half of life. We don't want to hear about a further journey beyond ego. We say, 'I will keep building my own house over and over again, thank you. I don't want it built for me. I will be in control of my journey. I will get

---

3 Cited in J. Singer, *Boundaries of the Soul: The Practice of Psychology*, New York: Anchor Press Doubleday, 1972, pp. 417–18.

the rewards of my own hard work, even if that work is killing me.' There can be a terrible self-defeating instinct in us, can there not?

We would love a short cut. We would love to be able to move seamlessly from a life of ego to a life of soul, and to be able to do this for ourselves. This is again our desire to be in control . . . and we cannot do it. We have to be taken there, usually kicking and screaming! We have to be given something, as Elijah on his escape into the wilderness was given food for the journey in the form of oatcakes and water. And perhaps we need to hear something.

John Eaton, in his appreciation of Psalm 81,[4] imagines a dramatic moment in the temple courts when God is acclaimed king at the autumn festival. There is an incredible noise of musical instruments and then silence. These words are dropped into that silence:

I heard a voice that I had not known:
'I relieved your shoulder of the burden;
  your hands were freed from the basket.' (Psalm 81.5b–6)

The people are taken back to the time of their slavery in Egypt. A choice is given: 'Will you listen and trust and receive my gifts, or will you continue in your slave mentality?' We are not very practised at being free men and women. 'We remember the fish we used to eat in Egypt for nothing, the cucumbers, the melons, the leeks, the onions, and the garlic' (Numbers 11.5). It is curious that the voice is described as 'a voice that I had not known'. Surely the voice of God is well known to his people? But perhaps the authentic voice of God is not so easy to recognize. We may spend a lifetime listening to sermons or preaching, trying to pray or teaching others to pray, searching for spiritual truth . . . and still the true voice of God will take us by surprise. Perhaps the voice of freedom is a voice we are not

---

4 John Eaton, *Psalms for Life*, London: SPCK, 2006, pp. 209–10.

used to hearing and do not really want to hear. We might just prefer to keep working by ourselves.

Or perhaps something does change, slowly . . . so slowly. We have passed through many stations and we have spent many frustrating hours in the waiting room hoping the next train will be along soon. And we might just reach the point where we know we have slipped up on more banana skins than we can count; we have totally lost faith in our own ego projects and have eventually worked out that surrender is much more fun than pushing. We will go on working, but we will want to work in a different way. We know God will always get there ahead of us, so we can be less anxious. Ego does not have to dance up and down inside us creating new, shiny, exciting plans for the future, for ego is now held in something much, much bigger.

12

Together

*Every now and then something happens in the hospice that will
pierce my soul. One day the husband of a patient on the hospice ward
wanted to talk with me. His wife had been admitted the day before
so the team did not yet know either of them very well. All I had heard
was that Sam had a history of mental health problems. I made tea
for both of us, invited him into my room and settled down to listen as
attentively as I could to what he wanted to say. Sam needed to talk
and talk and talk. He told me the whole story of his wife's diagnosis,
the very distressing times in hospital, the side-effects of treatment,
and how he was now at the end of his tether. He had been looking after her almost single-handedly for all of this time. Sam was
exhausted and without hope for the future. As we were talking, he
told me very calmly, 'When she dies, Padre, I'm going to kill myself.
I've got it all planned. It is the only way out of this situation. I know
I won't be able to live, when she goes. We are everything to each other.
How could I go on living without her? When I kill myself, we'll be
together for ever. It's the only way.' I had been listening peacefully to
all that Sam had been saying, but these words penetrated my carefully built defences. There was something profoundly shocking about
the calm way in which he talked of his suicide, and I felt as though
I had been knocked sideways. All of a sudden I felt extremely tired.
I found that my palms were sweaty and my face hot. I tried to think
about how to respond, feeling very responsible for this man and his
wife at this of time, weighed down by the burden of his pain. Willing
myself to open my mouth and respond, I acknowledged the pain of his
situation, and the isolation he must have been experiencing. I asked
about his plan to commit suicide, to see how well formulated it was.*

I then said I thought it would be a good idea if I could share what he had told me with other members of the team. I was dreading him refusing, but to my relief he agreed. This conversation happened before we employed a psychiatrist, so I talked first with our deputy matron and then with the consultant who was caring for Sam's wife. I was so grateful to be able to speak with my colleagues. As soon as I had told the story I felt better! I realized that this complex situation was not just my responsibility, but the responsibility of the whole multi-disciplinary team in the hospice, and others who had been caring for Sam and his wife before she came into the hospice. I was not alone with what Sam had disclosed to me. Fortunately, Sam had a good relationship with his GP, and over the next couple of weeks we found a way forward. I discovered again the importance of working in a team. I do not have to carry everything by myself.

In Chapter 3, we saw how *my way* can turn into *our way*, which in turn can be taken up into *the Way* which leads to life. We need to return to this theme once more. On the train, we sit on the seat reserved for us. We sit on our very own seat as the train takes us onwards through the day and the night, ever onwards, stopping at each station in turn (throwing us out into a few waiting rooms en route). It may feel as though we are the only person on this train, the only person who has travelled this way, and the only person who has experienced these particular experiences. We need to say very firmly to ourselves that this is not the whole truth. The journey is uniquely ours, but we are not alone on it. There is a great crowd of people, if only we could see and hear them, egging us on, urging us to 'stay with it'. They are fellow travellers who know this track as well as we do, and they tell us that we are all in this together.

Two different camps

We know this is true, but we are also very practised at putting ourselves into different compartments. In the hospice there is a boundary between those who are dying (patients) and those who are not dying (staff). The difference is accentuated by the wearing of uniforms by the nursing team and other professionals (which was insisted upon by the hospitals' trust a few years ago). But, of course, we are all dying. It's just that some of us are dying sooner than others. I attended an evening meeting at our wonderful Maggie's Centre[1] a little while ago. It was a meeting for those who were coming to terms with a terminal diagnosis together with their partners, with a group of professionals who could give practical advice on such issues as benefits, funeral planning and wills. I was struck by how divided we were. In one camp, were the patients and partners who were coming to receive something and in the other were the experts coming to give. The truth that was harder for us to acknowledge was that we are all frail human beings who will die, and that we need one other.

No privatized journey

It is likely that the psalm below was sung by pilgrims on the way up to the Temple before a festival lasting several days. I think it has something to teach us about community:

> O LORD, who may abide in your tent?
>   Who may dwell on your holy hill?
> Those who walk blamelessly, and do what is right,
>   and speak the truth from their heart;
> who do not slander with their tongue,
>   and do no evil to their friends,
>   nor take up a reproach against their neighbours
> in whose eyes the wicked are despised,
>   but who honour those who fear the LORD;
> who stand by their oath even to their hurt;

---

1 www.maggiescentres.org/our-centres/maggies-oxford

who do not lend money at interest,
    and do not take a bribe against the innocent.
Those who do these things shall never be moved. (Psalm 15)

If I am honest, I do not warm to these words. Here are rules about behaviour that do not speak of grace. I realize when I read the psalm that I have come to think of the Church as a community of sinners, of those who know their need of God, not a community for those who have passed some kind of moral test before they can come through the doors. But in the time when the psalms were first sung, it would be common practice for a sign to be displayed outside a temple telling the worshippers what behaviour was required of them. Because of my suspicion of law, I can miss the emphasis here on social responsibility and justice. The singer seems to be saying: 'It is not enough to come as an individual worshipper. We come as part of a community and therefore there are social obligations laid upon us. The right worship we will offer to God in the Temple flows out of our right relationships with our fellow human beings. We cannot lend money with exorbitant interest to someone who is in dire straits. We cannot accept a bribe so that an innocent person is convicted of a crime they did not commit. We must be aware of the tongue and the hurts we can inflict by the way we speak of others.' The psalmist tells us clearly that we sink or swim together. This is not our privatized journey to salvation. John Wesley once famously remarked that 'there is no such thing as a solitary Christian'.

Hospice as 'we'

In the hospice we have regular opportunities for those who have been bereaved to come together and remember their loved ones. People may be returning to the hospice for the first time since the death of their friend or family member, and these occasions are always full of the experience of loss.

When the invitations are sent out, a card 'leaf' is enclosed. Beautiful messages are written on these leaves which are then hung on a tree at the front of the gathering. Tea and cake is served, people talk to each other, poems are read and I usually tell a story and offer a blessing. The story I often tell is of 'Madipu'. I can't remember now where I first came across this story, but I know I have adapted it in the telling:

Madipu lives in an African village and knows that he is old and will die soon. He also knows that his extended family will find his death very hard to bear and wonders what he can do to gently prepare them. One morning Madipu goes around the village in the early morning collecting sticks. He moves very slowly and bends awkwardly. Soon a crowd of children is following him. 'Grandfather,' they shout, 'what are you doing?' He smiles, says nothing and continues on his slow journey. A few days later, the members of his family receive an invitation to a banquet, and they wonder what this banquet might be for. Speculation is intense. The day of the banquet comes, and everyone has a lovely time. There is plenty of food and drink. They dance to the beat of the drums and they tell each other stories. At the end of the banquet Madipu calls for quiet. He looks around at his family and says to them, 'You know that I am old, and I am about to die, but I do not wish you to be despairing in the face of my death.' They are quiet, except for one of his daughters who is quietly weeping. Madipu then produces some short sticks, all exactly the same length. He gives them out and invites everyone to break their stick in half. Everyone, including the youngest great-grandchild is able to do this easily. Then he produces bundles of sticks, about eleven or twelve, tied tightly with twine. 'Now,' says Madipu, 'see if you can break the sticks *now*.' And nobody, not even the strongest grandson, is able to break the bundle of sticks. 'This is how you must be in your grief,' he says. 'On your own you will be prey to fears, and loneliness, and much unhappiness. But

together you will help each other on the way. You will be
strong together, even though you grieve.'

Hospice as spiritual community

I love the song 'Brother, sister, let me serve you' by Richard
Gillard. It was one of the songs we sang at my welcome service
to the hospice. Here is one of the verses:

> We are pilgrims on a journey,
> and companions on the road;
> we are here to help each other
> walk the mile and bear the load.[2]

Helping will sometimes mean simply standing intentionally
with someone in their suffering. As Mary stood by the cross,
watching her son die, she did not wail or fall down to the
ground. She stood there, bearing the load with him. It is what
a hospice does. We do not take away a person's suffering, but
we try to reach out to be with her, so that she is not suffering
alone. Suffering is absorbed, anxiety and fear are held. This
is the meaning of a hospice as a spiritual community. It is not
spiritual by virtue of the spiritual beliefs of patients, family and
staff, but because we bear the load together.

I am aware of this keenly in our annual memorial service,
which we hold at Christmas time, called 'Lights of Love'. Up to
one thousand people come together in a car park of the Churchill
Hospital in Oxford to remember those who have died. Some
people have been coming for many years, and it has become part
of their Christmas ritual. Small cards, inscribed with words of
love, are laminated and attached to the Christmas tree; halfway

---

2 Richard Gillard, 'The Servant Song', © 1977, Universal music -
Brentwood Benson Publishing, www.songsolutions.org. All rights reserved. Used by permission.

through the service the Christmas tree lights are switched on. There is something very powerful about so many grieving people coming together in one place to remember. At the beginning, I invite people to turn around and shake the hand of someone they do not know. I hope that those who come by themselves know that they are not alone, for we need one another in these moments. We cannot make this journey alone.

Community and loss

Suffering can do two things to us. It turns us inwards or it turns us outwards, and most likely it will do both at different times. When I go into our day services in the hospice, I ask people how they are finding coming to this place. They will often tell me of the joy of being together with others, especially if they are alone at home. There is something reassuring about being with people who are 'in the same boat', who understand the journey without necessarily having to say anything. Something is understood which is beyond words. And I notice how caring people are. If someone does not attend, the others will ask about them. 'Is George OK? Is he unwell, or in hospital . . . he hasn't died, has he?' Of course, the challenging aspect of day services is that by being together with others who have a life-limiting illness, as someone observes another person becoming less well and dying, they find they are looking at their own deterioration and death. One of the most beautiful and painful things we do is to gather in the chapel/prayer room when someone has died, light a candle and remember. Lighting a candle is a prayer that needs no spoken words. We talk about the person who has died, and there is often laughter as we remember together. Together we experience heaviness and lightness, joy and deep sadness. We listen to some music as we think of the person and their family and how they have been part of this place and will be part of this place no more. One of the most real people I have ever known was a woman called Val who used to attend day services some years ago. Val was a concert pianist, and she would always come to these events, and with her stiff hands would play something beautiful on the piano that was exactly right for the person who had died. In these hard times of remembering, grace always comes to our aid. In sadness we are joined at the soul, and there is an unspoken unity between us which is very precious. We are looking at (apparent) separation and death, but we are together as we look. This is highly paradoxical, isn't it? We are discovering precious, fragile community in the midst of loss.

True community

Let us look now at how community comes about. In his book *The Different Drum*,[3] M. Scott Peck describes a process of community building, which he believes is the key to finding peace in our world. Out of his work with many groups, he outlines distinct stages that need to be experienced before community can be found. These are pseudo-community, chaos, emptiness and community. Pseudo-community is that very familiar state in which we are all nice to one another. This can happen easily in the life of the Church or a hospice. In this state we will go to great lengths not to offend one another. If there are things we do not agree with, we go along with them, and if there are people who offend us, we pretend they don't. There is the appearance of community, but no true intimacy. The chaos stage happens when people have the courage to speak up and say what they actually think and feel. There is a cacophony of different views, prejudices and opinions. Everyone is trying to convert everyone else to their way of thinking, and it can feel very uncomfortable! The temptation is to escape from this stage as quickly as possible and to find comfort again. One common way of doing this is through 'organizing out of chaos'. So we create

3   M. Scott Peck, *The Different Drum: the Creation of true Community – The First Step to World Peace*, London: Arrow Books, (1987) 1990.

some rules. For example, we agree that blue people will meet with other blue people for worship at 9.30 a.m. on Sundays, and green people will meet with the other green people at 11 a.m. There is another painful, healing possibility, however. And this concerns 'staying with it'. This will usually require a wise helper, because a group will find it hard to accomplish this move unaided. If a group can stay long enough in chaos, they might begin to hear the invitation to emptiness. It will usually require one or two people to speak honestly and vulnerably about how the chaos is affecting them. This honest speaking creates a different sort of space in which differences and prejudices fall away. The group no longer tries to fix or 'do' anything at all. The group members become empty of all striving. This creates a space for something new to come into being – true community.

In the context of a hospice, families and friends supporting a dying person may find community without too much trouble! The person in the bed who is dying may first experience the 'chaos' of different approaches to their dying. Some may want to chatter endlessly about day-to-day concerns and are nervous of being with someone who is dying, while others are comfortable in naming what is actually happening; some family members may think it's a good idea for someone to be there at the bedside all the time, while others think this is unnecessary. There may be concerns about how the person is being cared for. But the dying person herself may help the family group to move into the stage of 'emptiness', simply by being who she truly is in her dying. She has become so real in this time, almost radiant in her acceptance of grace, that she enables others to be real. There is no longer any nervousness or competition about how to help the dying person best. Egos stop their clamouring and a great simplicity falls on everyone. People do not have to speak, but when they do it seems to come from a deep place. Memories and laughter are shared and a quiet joy comes on everyone. Each feels they are part of the other. Christians will call this experience the fellowship of the Holy Spirit.

Prayer and community

I need to mention prayer in relation to community. The ex-centric practice of intercessory prayer is an important way in which we practise being together in suffering, joyful community. This is one of the most important prayers of the Church. The Othona Community[4] has a beautiful and simple way of praying for one another. On Thursday evenings the names of everyone who has been staying in the community during the previous week are read out. It's as simple as that. But as people sit in a circle and the names are dropped into the silence, it can be a time of profound communion. Sometimes there have been tensions between people, but in these moments we become one. We are no longer alone. I find I need different ways of praying for people, otherwise my prayer can become stale. I will sometimes sing out the names and concerns I have. The other day I found myself 'writing' the names of those I wanted to pray for on the palm of my hand with a ballpoint pen (point retracted!). I found this physical act very helpful. The people I was praying for seemed to become part of me.

The psalms remind us time and time again that we belong in community. The big danger for those following a religious or spiritual path is we think we are the only ones on that path. As we have seen, we too readily speak of 'my' journey. Some of us have an ambivalent relationship with the religious institutions to which we belong. But we do need the accountability, the fellowship and the safety of 'we'. I need to go to our annual ministerial synod and affirm that I still accept the teachings and discipline of the Methodist Church. We have seen how the singer of psalms knows nothing about the isolation of 'I', for this person is embedded in community, and their words are for the life of all. When one person sings, 'To you, O LORD, I lift up my soul' (Psalm 25.1), that person sings for the whole of Israel.

---

4 www.othona.org

We are kin

With just a little expanding of our national and ethnic horizons
we can intuit that we are all kin; we are all related to each other.
The person lying in a hospice bed, rushing to work, committing
an abusive act, desiring God, going on holiday, praying in the
mosque, shopping in the supermarket . . . is our sister or brother;
the same blood flows through our veins and the same God gives
us life and breath. We belong to each other. It is important that
when we reach out to care for another person, as in the example
at the beginning of this chapter, we know we cannot be alone.
When we listen to another person it can seem that we are there
carrying the whole situation by ourselves. But we bring with us
a host of people into that caring space. This will include our
family, friends, colleagues, our faith community and those who
support us through the difficult times. With a little bit of faith we
may even say it also includes some who have died, who still take
an interest in our life and continue to pray for us.

Precious unity

The separate, individual self is a very modern construction.
Our forebears would find our desire for autonomy strange and
laughable, for community has always been our truest identity:

> How very good and pleasant it is
>   when kindred live together in unity!
> It is like the precious oil on the head,
>   running down upon the beard,
> on the beard of Aaron,
>   running down over the collar of his robes.
> It is like the dew of Hermon,
>   which falls on the mountains of Zion.
> For there the LORD ordained his blessing,
>   life for evermore. (Psalm 133)

The singer sings these words as he looks out over the mass of pil-grims gathered at festival time in the temple courts. There is an experience of the beauty of the people of God coming together in this way, as one people. And they see how this unity is gift. For a Jewish man, a beard was a sign of maturity and wisdom. The first high priest, Aaron, was anointed for his high office and the singer in his imagination sees the oil liberally poured over Aaron's head, so that it runs down his long beard. But the flow of oil continues on to his robe, which would have been inscribed with the names of the 12 tribes of Israel.[5] This anointing, this blessing of God, therefore flows down over the whole people as the soft dew of the mighty snow-clad Mount Hermon flows down on to the crowd of worshippers assembled on the Temple Mount. The blessing covers the little ones as well as the great, and it covers the suffering ones as well as the comfortable.

We are definitely not on this train by ourselves, for there is a great crowd of pilgrims travelling with us. And the compan-ions who encourage us are not those who tell us what to do, or what to believe, or how to behave on the journey. Those who encourage us most are those who can look us in the eye and see through to our soul, and seeing what is there still reach out their hand to us. They stay with us, and their staying with us means we can stay with the journey too.

5 John Eaton, *Psalms for Life*, London: SPCK, 2006, p. 342.

Allowing the Journey

I have been running too hard and too long. Last week I presented at a conference, and while I was away our beloved dog was helped on her way to death. I allowed the tears of grief to flow. And now I have come to a quiet place. I slept well last night, wrapped in a deep, soft duvet. And this morning, as I sat watching the crows and the winter trees from my window, I slept again. I need to allow this healing sleep, not push my programme for this time. I need to allow God to touch my soul in his own way, to allow something to happen rather than to make something happen. I cannot make fruit.

When the LORD restored the fortunes of Zion,
    we were like those who dream.
Then our mouth was filled with laughter,
    and our tongue with shouts of joy;
then it was said among the nations,
    'The LORD has done great things for them.'
The LORD has done great things for us,
    and we rejoiced.
Restore our fortunes, O LORD,
    like the watercourses in the Negeb.
May those who sow in tears
    reap with shouts of joy.
Those who go out weeping,
    bearing the seed for sowing,
shall come home with shouts of joy,
    carrying their sheaves. (Psalm 126)

Sowing the seed is like a burial, and we know that some of the peoples around Israel performed mourning rituals as they scattered the seed on the ground. It is quite possible that Jesus' words about the dying grain, 'Unless a grain of wheat falls into the ground and dies . . . ' (John 12.24), picks up this ancient tradition. What a contrast there is between the sowing and the reaping; mourning becomes laughter and delight. But of course we need to notice again that there can be no reaping without the sowing of tears. The psalm comes from a time of national hardship, perhaps a severe drought. The singer recalls a similar crisis in the history of Israel when God restored their fortunes. And so the psalm is an appeal to the God of history and time to bring life again, as he did of old – to fill up his people with his loving kindness, as the dry waterbeds of the Negev overflow with water once more. The people mourn now, sowing the seed of futility and despair, but the time will come when God will send them out into the harvest fields to bring in the sheaves of corn. Then they shall dream again as their forefathers did when God rescued them from their distress. They will enter a different reality where God is all in all, which the New Testament calls the Kingdom of God. Richard Rohr is fond of calling this 'deep time'.

Allowing the process

When things go wrong for us, and we experience loss, darkness and failure, we may be tempted to dig up the seeds we have planted and burn them in our anger and our hurt. But in the economy of God loss and failure is not a waste. They are the ground out of which the new shoots of life can emerge. I will say it again. We can want so badly to make this happen ourselves. We want to prove we are OK, to prove we are capable, to prove we are not broken and vulnerable. But we cannot prove any of these things. All we can do is allow a process to happen within us, a process that often begins with the release of our tears.

In the hospice I have witnessed the shedding of many tears. Sometimes a person will be amazed by the quantity of tears it is possible to cry. And often (I am the same myself) a person will apologize for weeping. Why should we feel that, in the presence of distress, darkness and death we should need to say sorry for the expression of our pain and grief? It is so hard to allow the tears of our vulnerability, so hard to feel we are not in control of our emotions and our inner lives. But these tears water the seed that carries the potential for new life. Without the tears there could be no life and no harvest.

Finding a way through

There is always a way through for a distressed dying person and their family, although sometimes it is difficult for patients, families and staff to believe that. After all, when the active treatments have stopped there is palliation[1] in its many forms. Except in the most unusual of situations, there is always more symptom control that can be tried. But when patients and families are in the middle of distress and anguish, it is hard to see that. They see only the struggle – in the person who is dying and in their own hearts and souls. There will often be a very natural holding on to life. Sometimes I hear death referred to as 'The Inevitable'. The inevitability of death is something very hard for many of us to accept. We want to hold on to recovery, healing and life as our final destination.

---

1   The word palliation and the term palliative care come from the Latin word *pallium*, which means 'cloak'. Palliative care is a cloaking of symptoms so that they are no longer so troublesome. Spiritually we might think of being wrapped in the cloak of love.

I remember a young woman, Amanda, who was dying slowly in the hospice. She had been married to her equally young husband, Dave, for just a year. They wanted all possible active treatments for as long as possible. Dave and Amanda's parents wanted to be with her most of the time, to help her as much as they could through this stressful time. I came to know them all well, and although not regular churchgoers, they were people of deep faith. They wanted me to join my prayers to theirs for a miracle for Amanda. They could not envisage her death, as this would have felt like a betrayal, and her survival was the only possible way forward; anything else was an impossibility. I felt very awkward when they first asked me to pray for her healing. I knew that the medical prognosis was not good, and that Amanda was dying. Equally, I did not want to rip hope away from a family who were distressed beyond words. My compromise was to pray for wholeness, peace and inner strength for Amanda and for all of her family and friends. The days passed, and Amanda became weaker and weaker. She slept a lot of the time. On one particular day, the family had a conversation with a doctor who confirmed, very gently and compassionately, that Amanda was dying and might well be dying quite soon. This was incredibly hard for all of them to hear, but something changed for them on that day. They had been holding out for life, while seeing deterioration and dying. Now, as well as the pain of having to face the death of the one they loved, there was also relief. They could stop pretending and face the reality of the situation they were in. Instead of praying for a miracle, they surrounded Amanda with all of their love. They spoke their love to her, and she spoke her love back to them. They laughed and cried over their memories. They were able to accompany her in her dying, in a way that was very beautiful to witness. The pain of loss was almost tangible in the room, but they had found a true way to travel on, a way of love. This was not the path any of them had chosen, but it was a path that they were now beginning to accept.

I can't

One of the hardest things is to allow the journey of our life to be as it has been. I am not proud of some of the stations I have stopped at, and I would love to be able to change my history. I cannot – and I still find this so frustrating. I want to rewrite the past, turn the clock back, be a different person than the actual person I was and make different choices than the choices I made. It is so hard for me to accept that I would not be the person I am now without the painful, unravelling times . . . that in some sense sin and brokenness were necessary. I want the rules to be different. I want to avoid the apparent necessity of falling. If I had my time over again, I would still want to go straight to the harvest without the sowing of tears! And I also know that these words come from my ego, who does not want to admit that the new orientation only comes out of dying in some form or other.

It is Christmas time and I look at the familiar nativity scene on the table in the hospice chapel. I find myself looking at Mary, and I imagine what she might say to me. Mary talks to my inner child who is afraid. She says that when the angel visited her, all she could do was to summon up all her courage and allow God's grace to work. The fear is about not being able to control outcomes. She couldn't. I can't. What I can do is to make a conscious decision to allow something to happen that I have no control over.

The seed grows

It is sometimes very hard to believe that any change or growth will happen in our lives. It seems that all is darkness. The lights in the carriage go out, and we feel alone again. At times like these, how can we leave the seed in the ground and believe that it will grow? Jesus tells this story:

'The kingdom of God is as if someone would scatter seed on the ground, and would sleep and rise night and day, and the seed would sprout and grow, he does not know how.' (Mark 4.26–27)

When it is hard to believe the seed is growing, we may remember, if we can, as Israel remembered (we explored this a little in Chapter 6). She remembered that God had brought deliverance before, and if God had brought deliverance before, then God could do it again. For us, we can only wait until something shifts. We cannot work our own transformation. We cannot give birth to ourselves. We cannot make new life appear through wishful thinking or magical prayer. This waiting means a radical surrender, a giving up of effort and struggling. We let it be. We allow the seed, watered with our tears, to lie there in the ground. And when the green shoot pokes its head out of the ground we can praise God, for this is his work of restoration and new life, and his alone.

We have rattled our way to the last station of the book, and in some ways it does not seem a very satisfactory way to end. But perhaps that is the whole point. The carriage we are sitting in will probably have a crisp packet stuffed down the seat and a drinks can rolling around on the floor. But we are still on the train, and perhaps that is all that matters.

Postscript

These words were written by Lorraine Long in the last weeks of her life at Sobell House and were found in a notebook after she had died. They were read out at her funeral:

We are all on the train of life. For some, the journey is short, but for most of us the journey is long. Sometimes the journey is smooth and happy like a train to the seaside. Excitement, happiness, being with loved ones and meeting new people.

We like the train to stop from time to time so we can get off, stretch our legs and enjoy new cultures, food and local traditions. We enjoy it as our journey stretches out and we delay getting to the last station. As the journey continues we get older and wiser but sometimes everything starts to wear us out.

Sometimes we want to stop the delays and get to that final station.

I have reached the point where the journey is exhausting, and I want the delays to become shorter. The views from the train are good some days but become bleaker on others.

The people around me are just as loving, loved and fun to be with, but they have more energy and enthusiasm to carry on with the exciting trip with glorious views, fantastic fun and experiences.

I think it will soon be time for me to find a station where I can disembark, relax, unwind and find peace and quiet.

Thank you, my loved ones, my friends and the many people who have given me strength on my hard final trip. I have enjoyed my journey of life and couldn't have done it without you.

P.S. For all of you who know me well, my train is travelling at a relaxed and quiet pace not at high speed. I have always liked a clear view and not a blur of hedges.

Further Reading

The challenge of suffering

Harold S. Kushner, *When Bad Things Happen to Good People*, New York: Anchor Books (1981) 2004.

Henri Nouwen, *Turn my Mourning into Dancing: Finding Hope in Hard Times*, Nashville, TN: W Publishing Group, 2001.

John A. Sanford, *Ministry Burnout*, Ramsey, NJ: Paulist Press, 1982.

Margaret Silf, *The Other Side of Chaos: Breaking through When Life is Breaking Down*, Chicago, IL: Loyola Press, 2011.

Margaret Spufford, *Celebration: A Story of Suffering and Joy*, London: Mowbray (1989) 1996.

John Swinton, *Raging with Compassion: Pastoral Responses to the Problem of Evil*, Grand Rapids, MI: Eerdmans, 2007.

Philip Yancey, *Where is God When it Hurts?*, London: Marshall Pickering (1977) 1991.

Frances Young, *Arthur's Call*, London: SPCK, 2014.

Death and dying

Sheila Cassidy, *Sharing the Darkness: The Spirituality of Caring*, Markyknoll, NY: Orbis Books (1988) 1991.

Sioned Evans and Andrew Davison, *Care for the Dying: A Practical and Pastoral Guide*, Norwich: Canterbury Press, 2014.

Marie de Hennezel, *Intimate Death: How the Dying Teach Us to Live*, trans. Carol Brown Janeway, London: Little, Brown and Company, 1997.

David Kuhl, *What Dying People Want: Practical Wisdom for the End of Life*, New York: Public Affairs, 2002.

Steve Nolan, *Spiritual Care at the End of Life: The Chaplain as a Hopeful Presence*, London and Philadelphia: Jessica Kingsley, 2012.

Christina M. Puchalski, *A Time for Listening and Caring: Spirituality and the Care of the Chronically Ill and Dying*, New York: Oxford University Press, 2006.

Kathleen Dowling Singh, *The Grace in Dying: How We are Transformed Spiritually as We Die*, San Francisco, CA: HarperSanFrancisco, 1998.

Irvin D. Yalom, *Staring at the Sun: Overcoming the Terror of Death*, San Francisco, CA: Jossey-Bass, 2008.

Spirituality

Geiko Müller-Fahrenholz, *The Art of Forgiveness*, Geneva: WCC Publications, 1997.

Henri J. M. Nouwen, *The Return of the Prodigal Son*, London: Darton, Longman and Todd, 1994.

Richard Rohr, *Breathing Underwater: Spirituality and the Twelve Steps*, Cincinnati, OH: Franciscan Media, 2011.

Richard Rohr, *Falling Upwards: A Spirituality for the Two Halves of Life*, San Francisco, CA: Jossey-Bass, 2011.

Mark Townsend, *The Gospel of Falling Down: The Beauty of Failure in an Age of Success*, Winchester and New York: O Books, 2007.

W. H. Vanstone, *The Stature of Waiting*, London: Darton, Longman and Todd, 1982.

Psalms

William P. Brown, *Seeing the Psalms: A Theology of Metaphor*, Louisville, KY: Westminster John Knox Press, 2002.

Walter Brueggemann, *The Message of the Psalms: A Theological Commentary*, Minneapolis, MN: Augsburg, 1984.

Walter Brueggemann, *Spirituality of the Psalms*, Minneapolis, MN: Augsburg, 2002.

John H. Eaton, *Psalms*, London: SCM Press, 1967.

John H. Eaton, *Psalms for Life*, London: SPCK, 2006.

Simon P. Stocks, *Using the Psalms for Prayer through Suffering*, Cambridge: Grove Books, 2007.

Bereavement

Marian Carter, *Dying to Live: A Theological and Practical Workbook on Death, Dying and Bereavement*, London: SCM Press, 2014.

Tom Gordon, *New Journeys Now Begin: Learning on the Path of Grief and Loss*, Glasgow: Wild Goose Publications, 2006.

C. S. Lewis, *A Grief Observed*, London: Faber and Faber, 1961.

Reflecting with our 'shadow selves'

Bob Whorton, *Reflective Caring: Imaginative Listening to Pastoral Experience*, London: SPCK, 2011.